Pathways to Praying with Teens

Pathways to Praying with Teens

Maryann Hakowski

Saint Mary's Press
Christian Brothers Publications
Winona, Minnesota

To my mother, Cecylia,
to Beth, Jude, Barbara, Andre, Pat,
and all the many women
who taught me how to pray
and who nurtured my spirituality.

The publishing team included Robert P. Stamschror, development editor; Susan Baranczyk, copy editor; Amy Schlumpf Manion, production editor and typesetter; Jayne Stokke, cover designer; Elaine Kohner, illustrator; pre-press, printing, and binding by the graphics division of Saint Mary's Press.

The acknowledgments continue on page 94.

Printed in the United States of America

Printing: 9 8 7 6 5 4 3 2 1

Year: 2001 00 99 98 97 96 95 94 93

ISBN 0-88489-296-4

Contents

Introduction

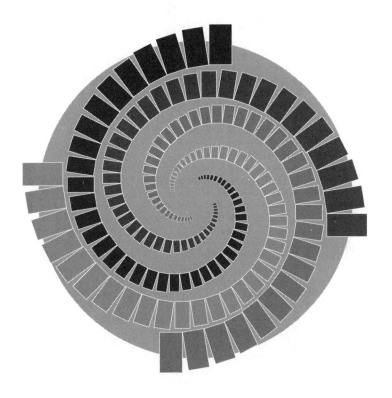

God . . .
are you there?
I've been taught
and told I ought
to pray.
But the doubt
won't go away;
yet neither
will my longing to be heard.
My soul sighs
too deep for words.
Do you hear me?
God . . .
are you there?

This excerpt from a poem by Ted Loder sums up how many teens feel about prayer, and for that matter how many adults feel about it also. Prayer is something we are taught to do, something we are told to do, something we need to do, yet something that can be so very hard to do.

When I ask teens, "What is prayer?" the most common response is, "Talking to God." Yet it isn't all that simple. We need to know how to approach God, how to figure out what to say, and then how to listen for the response.

Put Away the Paste

Prayer cannot be pasted onto anyone's life. It needs to take root and grow.

Prayer is a process. It cannot be a once-and-done event. I have seen high school religion teachers squeeze in a three-hour retreat to fulfill a course requirement and youth group leaders throw together a quickie youth Mass to claim a spiritual component to their program. These events hardly ever make the grade as real prayer experiences. Prayer experiences for young people need to be well thought out and planned. They need to have their own integrity and yet be incorporated into a variety of activities.

The starting point for prayer with teens is right where they are at in their spirituality. You may have to begin slowly; then again, you may discover that the teens are already close to God in their own way. Never assume that young people aren't in touch with God. They may know God in ways that you do not.

Prayer Is a Verb

Alla Renée Bozarth is well known for her poem "God is a Verb." I want to borrow from her analogy but change it to say, "Prayer Is a Verb."

Verbs are active. They do not sit around all day waiting for nouns to do something. Get the young people involved in planning prayer, leading prayer, and participating in the prayer experience. They may need some guidance at first, but they really get into it when they have permission to be creative. The times I have seen teens most excited by prayer is when they have been involved in the entire experience—start to finish.

Have some fun; use your imagination. Avoid the temptation to always copy a ready-made prayer service, just switching the readings around now and then. Try new resources, root around in your supply closet, listen to the Top 10 on the radio, and before you know it, you will be finding prayer ideas in all sorts of places.

Prayer is a way for young people—and everyone—to reach out and touch God in their life. It is a bridge between God and God's people on earth. Be a bridge builder.

Be Open to Change

Prayer does not change God; rather, it changes us, who offer the prayer.

So often we aim our "gimmie" prayers at God, expecting God to do something or change something for us, and then we get angry when God doesn't come through. Teens do this too. Quite a few times I have heard the refrain, "Well, I prayed to God, but nothing happened."

But while prayer does not always change the situation one is praying about, prayer can indeed change the person. While you are helping teens discover this, you will, no doubt, also see change in yourself. A good prayer life is ongoing, and change brought about by prayer, likewise, is ongoing. We need to help teens hope for, look for, and see this effect of prayer in themselves and in the world around them, especially in their relationships with others.

What Is Inside This Book?

Each of chapters 1 through 11 in this book focuses on a particular form of prayer and is divided into four parts: an overview, guidelines, prayer starters, and a complete prayer service.

The *overview* presents my experience with the form of prayer, followed by *guidelines* for using the form.

The *prayer starters* are ideas to get you started in planning your own prayer experiences. You can use one of the prayer starters and expand upon it or combine two or more as building blocks for a whole prayer service.

The *complete prayer service* serves both to illustrate the form of prayer described in the chapter and to provide you with a ready-made prayer service if you wish to use it.

Chapter 12, on miscellaneous prayer, is an exception to the format of the other chapters, offering an array of creative prayer suggestions that don't seem to fit in any of the other categories in this book.

Since all of the prayer forms in the book have some aspects in common, you will likely see prayer starters for some forms that can easily be used for other forms. You will notice, too, that the prayer service illustrating the use of one prayer form always includes other forms of prayer.

The perspective of prayer that I have in offering the variety of prayer forms in this book is broad. It encompasses the actual act of praying as well as experiences that have the potential to move one to prayer.

Prayer Is an Adventure

Throughout the writing of this book, I have kept with me a "prayer idea" journal made by some teens attending a retreat. It became special as I weaved notes from the journal into the pages and chapters of this book, but it was special also because of the way the teens had decorated it. They had cut out words and pictures that describe prayer as talk, sacred places, surprising, reaching out and blessing someone, rejoicing, looking toward the horizon, family, news, the Bible, ahead of its time, nurturing, and adventure. All of these words and symbols helped enrich the meaning of prayer as I wrote. But the one that I hope comes through the strongest in the prayer forms that I describe for you is the word *adventure!*

Adventure can be defined as an exciting and remarkable experience. That is what I hope these prayer forms provide for you and your young people.

Are you unsure of whether you have the faith it takes to embark on this adventure of youth and prayer? Let's borrow the three tests of faith from the movie *Indiana Jones and the Last Crusade* to find out:

Indiana Jones has climbed mountains, outsmarted treasure hunters, and even endured snakes to find the precious treasures he seeks. You might say that you aren't impressed because he hasn't spent an entire weekend with a youth group or taken a fourteen-hour bus trip to a teen youth convention.

Yet in his quest for the Holy Grail, the chalice of Christ, Indy must meet three tests of faith. These tests of faith hold a lot of truth for anyone who works with youth and certainly anyone who prays with them and for them.

The First Test of Faith

The first test of faith is *The Penitent Person Will Pass.* Indy learns that kneeling before God is the only way to keep his head while sharp blades swirl around him.

When approaching prayer with youth, we must first remember that God is the focus of prayer and ask God's guidance. We need to be humble and allow God to work through us in reaching out to the teens. Work on your own prayer life before helping the teens work on theirs. You and God together can do a much better job than if you try to go it alone.

The Second Test of Faith

The second test of faith is *Walking in the Footsteps of the Word.* Indiana Jones has great motivation to follow in the footsteps of God's word: he is fearful of falling into a ravine. But walking in the footsteps of the word of God is advice that can be well taken by you as you approach youth and prayer. If you yourself fall in love with the Scriptures, that love is sure to be contagious in working and praying with the teens.

The Third Test of Faith

The third test of faith is the hardest challenge. Near the end of Indy's adventure, a giant chasm is the only thing left between him and the Holy Grail. His only choice is to pull strength from within himself and take a giant *Leap of Faith.* You can read hundreds of books and spend hours in preparation for a prayer experience with young people, but eventually you just have to trust yourself, and your God, and just do it.

> But don't worry.
> You have it in you.
> Simply close your eyes and . . . jump!

1
Symbols:
Allowing Images to Speak to Us and for Us

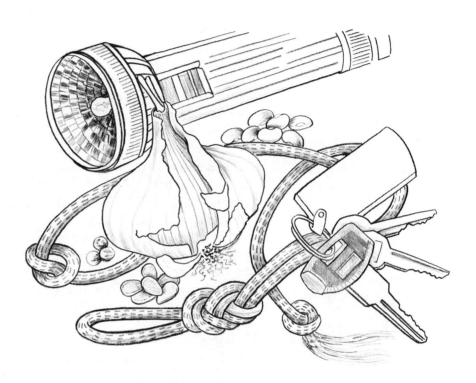

Overview

Symbols have a power just waiting to be tapped in youth ministry, especially in the creation of exciting, inviting prayer experiences. Praying only with words and thoughts can be abstract and uninvolving; using symbols and images can stir up the imagination, and interest and excite us. Young people are used to having symbols do this for them. They experience symbols and images in almost every place they look—church, school, home, and all the forms of media in popular culture.

One of my first experiences of the richness of symbols in prayer occurred during a master's seminar in college. The professor asked everyone in the widely diverse class to take out an index card and a pack of crayons. She said she would give us a word and we were to draw the first thing that came into our mind. The word was "God." The surprising thing was that I didn't draw a cross or a heart or anything quite ordinary, but a giant burst of fireworks.

Later, when I thought about it, I realized that I saw God as both powerful and beautiful. What was more amazing was the incredible array of symbols that had come forth from the group. I now use a variation of this activity with some of my retreat groups. Their symbols tell me a lot about where they are at in their spirituality.

One of my favorite activities is to give teens some clay and see where their imagination leads them. When expressing their view of God in this medium, there is rarely duplication, even in a large group. The teens laugh at first, then become intrigued. They especially like the opportunity to look at all the other creations.

Using symbols in prayer can

- open a window to help teens experience traditional church symbols in a new way or expand on the symbols' meaning
- help teens discover the God-centered messages hidden in the symbols in popular culture
- give teens permission to use their imagination and allow them to approach God in different ways
- put surprise and a sense of fun into prayer experiences, when teens often expect the ordinary, formula prayer services
- enable teens to think and experience things in a manner that does not require words

Recently, I went on a retreat for myself. (Retreat directors should really do this more often.) While the entire retreat was well done, the most moving part was a foot-washing ceremony. I had read the scriptural account of foot-washing (John 13:1–14) before and had seen it done in liturgy, but I had never experienced it myself. Especially moving was the fact that one of my mentors in ministry was the one who washed my feet. No words can express the impact that the experience of this symbol has had on my understanding of my ministry.

Guidelines

1. Choose the symbols first and then build a prayer service around them, so that music, prayer, and scriptural readings support the symbols rather than take away from them.
2. Allow the teens to choose or identify their own symbols from popular culture. Stay in touch with youth culture and the symbols found there that can teach us.
3. Do not use too many symbols at one time. This can be confusing and blur the symbols' power. If you do use more than one symbol, make sure the symbols work together, or are tied together by the theme of the prayer service or a scriptural reading.
4. Never directly tell the teens what a symbol means. Symbols are meant to be experienced, not defined.
5. Challenge the teens to find more than one meaning or different levels of meaning for each symbol.
6. Offer opportunities in large or small groups for the young people to share the insights they get from experiencing the symbols. Be prepared for some surprises.
7. Make sure you tell the teens that it is okay if they do not find the same meaning in a symbol as others do. Everyone is different and sees symbols in different ways.

8. Encourage the teens to experience symbols with as many senses as will respond. Let the young people not only see a symbol but touch it, listen to it, smell it, and in some cases taste it as well.

Sometimes a symbol can touch someone in a way that little else can. I remember one young man who did his best during an entire overnight retreat to fight everything we did. He was uncooperative and often disruptive. Even his classmates grew tired of his antics. He would often wait to catch my eye before doing something inappropriate.

Just when I felt like I was at the end of my rope, he became fascinated by a simple prayer using a marble. Not only did he ask me all about it, but a few weeks later I received an envelope in the mail from him—with a marble inside.

Prayer Starters

1. Pass a simple wooden cross around a circle of youth gathered for prayer. Dim the lights. Ask the teens each to hold the cross for a minute, to touch it and look at it. Ask them to share one word that comes to mind when they think of Christ crucified.
2. Use an evergreen branch as a springboard for prayer on the theme "God's love is everlasting." A small piece of the branch may later be used to bless the young people with holy water.
3. If several different groups of young people are gathering together for prayer, ask each group to bring some holy water from their church. Gather the holy water in a large bowl as a sign of unity in Christ. The young people can bless themselves or each other with the water.
4. Use a spider plant as part of a prayer service based on the passage "'I am the vine, and you are the branches'" (John 15:5). When the spider plant grows, it forms complete miniature plants attached to the main one. We too are independent yet part of the main vine, Jesus Christ.
5. At the start of a penance service or a talk on sin, give each person a piece of rope tied in many knots. To talk about the effect of sin on the community, use a single long rope tied in many knots.
6. For the topic of the value of material possessions versus the value of personal talents, ask each person to bring a prized possession from home and contrast it with a personal talent or skill. Or take a VCR, a CD player, a Walkman, designer jeans, and the like, and pile them on one side of the room. Place a candle and a crucifix on the other side.
7. Start a prayer service completely in the dark. Read scriptural passages about light and faith, increasing the light in the room with each reading. This can be done with a number of candles or various types of lamps or flashlights.
8. Give each person a seed to hold while reading and reflecting on the parable of the sower and the seed (Mark 4:1–9).
9. Ask the teens to leave their shoes outside the door before entering a room for a prayer service on homelessness or any other theme for which you want them to "walk in the shoes of another."

10. Ask each person to wear a mask for a prayer service in October, near Halloween. Challenge the teens to "take off their mask" at a prayer service on "being yourself."
11. Create a giant banner with a picture of an hourglass and the saying "Now is the time for God." Ask each member of your group to sign his or her name on a small circular sticker. During prayer, each person can come forward and place the sticker on the hourglass part of the banner as a promise to make time for God in his or her life.
12. Plan a prayer service about dealing with tough times, centering around the saying "Life is like an onion: you peel off one layer at a time, and sometimes you cry."
13. Choose one symbol and challenge different groups of teens to plan a prayer service based on it. Combine the best ideas from each group into one prayer service.
14. Ask each person to take an item from their pocket or desk. Spread out all the items on the floor or on a large table and see what prayers result from everyone's meditating on common objects.
15. During Advent, ask the teens to cut out a paper ornament in the shape of an object that represents themselves and then to write a prayer on the ornament. Have them place their ornament on an evergreen tree during the prayer of the faithful at liturgy.
16. Collect several objects that represent different countries. During a prayer for world peace, remember each country and its people by name as an object is placed before the altar.
17. Borrow a giant ring of keys from the parish janitor for a prayer service on finding "the keys to the Kingdom of God." When the teens leave, give each one a construction-paper key that says, "Jesus is the key."
18. Give each person a large rock at the start of a reconciliation service based on the passage "I will remove from your body the heart of stone and give you a heart of flesh" (Ezek. 36:26, NRSV).
19. Invite a priest who works with people who are hearing impaired to come and celebrate Mass in sign language. Teach the teens how to sign a prayer, perhaps the Lord's Prayer.
20. Pray the Lord's Prayer, stop after the phrase "Give us this day our daily bread," and break homemade bread with each other.
21. Place a bowl of M&M's in the center of the prayer space. Ask each person to take a handful and share a reflection on individuality and how it is possible to be different and yet the same.
22. Share with the teens the significance of prayer shawls in the Jewish faith. During a prayer service, ask the teens to come forward one at a time, place a shawl on their shoulders, and lead the group in prayer.
23. During an affirmation service, sprinkle a little bit of salt in each person's hand and say, "'You are the salt of the earth'" (Matt. 5:13, NRSV).
24. Use the sign of the cross as the center of a prayer service. Divide the prayer service into four parts: "In the Name of the Father," "And of the Son," "And of the Holy Spirit," and "Amen."

25. Try to borrow an old stop sign from the department of transportation in your area, or use a life-size one you've created yourself. Place the stop sign in the center of your circle for a prayer service on things that stop us from getting closer to God.

Prayer Service "Prayer in a Backpack"

Featuring the Use of Symbols

In addition to symbols, other prayer forms found in this prayer service are music, quiet prayer, scriptural prayer, and shared prayer.

Themes found in this prayer service are journey, discipleship, and discernment.

Supplies

Ten index cards; a pen; a hole punch; a ball of string; a Walkman; a watch; a piece of jewelry; a mirror; a teddy bear; a dollar; scissors; a calculator; a backpack; a small table; road maps; white paper; glue; light green paper; the song "Come and Journey with Me," by David Haas; a Bible; pencils; a recording of "Do You Know Where You're Going To?" by Diana Ross; a tape player or CD player; a basket

Preparation

Write each of the following "backpack prayers" on an index card and attach it with string to the symbol designated in brackets following the prayer.
1. "Lord, help us to tune out the many distractions in our lives and find quiet to listen to you." [Walkman]
2. "Lord, help us to slow down the hectic pace we set. Teach us how to make time for you." [Watch]
3. "Lord, keep us from wanting more and more possessions and putting things before people." [Piece of jewelry]
4. "Lord, help us to accept your life plan for us instead of always telling you where we want to go and be." [Map]
5. "Lord, help us to look inside each person for you instead of always being concerned about outward appearances." [Mirror]
6. "Lord, give us the courage to set aside our insecurities and be willing to take risks in order to follow you." [Teddy bear]
7. "Lord, help us to realize that the things of real value in life are not measured by how much they cost." [Dollar]
8. "Lord, help us to set aside any grudges or petty jealousies that tangle up our hearts. Show us that you are the tie that binds." [Ball of string]
9. "Lord, help us to cut out our bad habits and dependencies and learn how to depend only on you." [Scissors]
10. "Lord, help us not to put facts and figures before faith. Teach us to believe even when we cannot see." [Calculator]

Place the symbols and cards in a backpack and put the pack on a small table in the center of the prayer circle, where all can see it.

Cut road maps into 4-by-4-inch pieces and glue a 3-by-3-inch piece of white paper into the center of each map piece, to provide space for the teens to write a petition.

Make a copy of the closing prayer for each person. As a background for the words, photocopy a road map on light green paper using a light exposure setting.

If your available songbooks do not include the closing song, find the song elsewhere, write for copyright permission, and include the words on the sheet with the closing prayer.

Ask for volunteers to read the backpack prayers, but do not let them remove the symbols from the backpack or read the prayers ahead of time.

Ask a teen to prepare to do the scriptural reading.

Give each person a pencil, a map piece, and a green prayer sheet as she or he arrives for prayer.

Procedure

Call to prayer

Opening song: "Do You Know Where You're Going To? (Theme from *Mahogany*)" by Diana Ross

Reading: Mark 10:17–27 (the rich man)

Pause for quiet reflection

Backpack prayer: Invite each volunteer to pull a symbol and its attached card from the backpack, hold the symbol so all can see what it is, and then read the prayer found on the card.

If time permits, ask the teens to think of other symbols that could have been included in the backpack and to write their own accompanying prayers.

Road map petitions: Request that each person write a brief prayer of petition on their map piece, asking God to guide them on the journey of life ahead. When everyone has finished, direct them to place the petitions in a basket.

If your group has access to a chapel, place the basket of map petitions in the chapel before the Blessed Sacrament and ask the teens to stop in each day for a week and pray one of the petitions.

Closing prayer: To close the prayer service, ask everyone to read the following prayer:

> Lord, help us to accept your invitation to "come and follow me."
> Shield us from doubt, so we never put anything or anyone before you.
> Help us to unpack all the things
> that put distance between you and ourselves.
> Guide us on our journey
> so we may follow in your footsteps
> on the way to your Father.
> Amen!

Closing song: "Come and Journey with Me," by David Haas

2
Music:
Messages in the Melodies

Overview

Once, when I was desperately looking for a song to fit a prayer service, I looked through all my tapes and pored over the Top 10 countdown for the week. Even browsing through the racks at the local record store did not seem to help.

The day before the retreat, I still needed just the right song to end the prayer service. As I was finishing preparations for my trek to the retreat center and was juggling my belongings into my car—still worried about the prayer service—I turned on the car radio to the song "Send Me an Angel," by Scorpions. Perfect! Ask me if I believe in the Holy Spirit.

Music often speaks to us in the midst of our life experiences and helps us find meaning in what we are going through. Music can help teens put into words the things they cannot say themselves. It is a language they speak, understand, and respond to.

Music can
- build a bridge between popular culture and faith in God
- open up avenues to help teens understand themselves and their relationships with others

- help teens realize they are not alone in their troubles and offer them a way to express their feelings
- give texture to the ritual of young people's prayer and a link to the way the rest of the faith community prays
- set a special tone or atmosphere for prayer
- bridge generation gaps, because music has been an important part of adolescence through the years

I have often been surprised by the type of music that reaches teens. I make an extra effort to stay current with the music of today and read up on the recording artists making the news. Yet, when teens are asked to choose their own music, they often pull favorites from the record racks of their parents.

One artist that has managed to cross at least the last generation gap is Billy Joel. I find it amazing that a singer I listened to when I was in high school still has messages for today's teens.

One time, on a retreat, the scheduled program for the evening finished early, and the young people asked to have a dance. We moved all the tables in the cafeteria, found a music box with large speakers, and sent the teens to their dorm rooms to collect their favorite tapes.

We listened to a lot of music that night, but I will never forget how the evening ended: The dancing had died down, and Billy Joel's *Greatest Hits* was playing. I joined the teens in singing "Allentown" and "Piano Man." They knew every single word. And so did I.

Guidelines

1. Give the music of teens a chance, even if it is not your own. Listen to it; find out what is on the Top 10. Tap the music's potential for prayer and discussion.
2. Be willing to experiment with a variety of both religious music and popular music that appeals to the teens. I have always enjoyed singing, but I can remember growing to dread the song "Though the Mountains May Fall," by Dan Schutte, because we sang it at every liturgy and prayer service when I was in high school. A little variety would have saved that high school music program.
3. Whenever possible, let the teens choose their own music for prayer and liturgy.
4. Invite teens who play instruments to share their talents at prayer. Perhaps a flute solo could add to meditation time. A trumpet could herald a call to prayer.
5. Try to use live music whenever possible, but use tapes or CDs if no one is available to play for your group. The publishers or distributors of most current parish songbooks have recordings available, and the teens are usually eager to bring in their own music.
6. When selecting songs to sing, try to find songs that have a comfortable voice range for both men and women.
7. Use a mixture of new songs and ones familiar to the teens. Teach new songs, but not too many all at once. Make the words available in songbooks or on songsheets.
8. Obtain copyright permission from the music publisher when you copy the words of a song onto a handout for the teens.

9. Invite teens to be leaders of song. Encourage everyone to join in singing at liturgy, but do not try to force it.

10. Advocate for a good overall parish music program. Good parish music programs often yield teens who enjoy singing. I was awed by the harmonies sung by one parish youth group at a retreat Mass. I learned later that many of the members had been involved in church choirs from an early age and that their congregation at Sunday Mass was enthusiastic about singing.

Some adults in the parish may have to be convinced about the value of using modern music in prayer. When participating in the prayer service found in this chapter, a priest who had been invited to hear confessions was visibly upset by the excerpts of modern music we were using. Later, he remarked several times about how unusual it was for so many teens to choose to receive the sacrament of reconciliation. He was a reluctant convert, but he realized that the music had something to do with it.

Prayer Starters

1. Play music to set the tone while the teens gather for prayer. For example, play "Material Girl," by Madonna, before a prayer service on materialism.

2. Introduce the teens to a different culture by teaching them a song in a foreign language. Try singing the refrain of a song in Spanish or French and the verses in English.

3. Use the refrain of a well-known song as the response to psalm verses such as those used in the Mass. Ask various teens to read the verses.

4. As a prayer service, alternate verses of one song with readings, reflection, or shared prayer.

5. Challenge the teens to put together a prayer service incorporating music from the Top 10 songs of the week.

6. Find an MTV video in which the lyrics of the song do not match the message given by the video images. Contrast the lyrics with the message given by the images.

7. Use several snippets of current songs to create a musical collage on how much God loves us.

8. Compare some modern music with readings from the Psalms. Find parallel themes between popular music and the Psalms. Share with the teens that the Psalms were the popular music of an ancient day.

9. Ask the teens to go through the songs in the Glory and Praise series and *Peoples Mass Book* and list their "Top 10" church songs.

10. Allow the teens to choose an appropriate contemporary song for the Communion meditation during liturgy.

11. Ask a local dance instructor to help the teens learn a liturgical dance to a popular song.

12. For a series of parent-teen programs, ask both generations to bring in songs about intergenerational relationships that they would like to share during a prayer service. Examples are "Cat's in the Cradle," by Harry Chapin, and "No Son of Mine," by Genesis.

13. Ask the teens to hunt for contemporary songs with specific references to the Bible hidden within them.
14. If the teens in your class or group are unfamiliar with Christian rock, arrange for them to attend a concert. Later, discuss how it may have been a prayerful experience. Ask the teens to contrast it with other concerts they have attended.
15. Invite a parish bell choir to do a workshop for your group. The choir could perform a few songs and teach the youth how to play a simple melody.
16. Use music as props and aids for young people who give witness talks about their faith. Songs can help them express the faith experiences they have had in their life.

Modern Songs with a Message

Modern songs with a message can be particularly effective when used with appropriate activities, such as the witness talks mentioned above or prayer services. Listening to the songs ahead of time to make sure they fit the occasion is important. Here are examples of modern songs with a message, along with the message each contains:

"Love Takes Time," by Mariah Carey: If you listen carefully to "Love Takes Time" you can hear the parable of the prodigal son (Luke 15:11–32).

After taking half of his father's wealth and squandering it, the prodigal son sits among the pigs and sings, "I had it all but I let it slip away." He realizes what he has done to his father and wants to go home: "I was blind to let you go; I can't escape the pain inside. . . . I don't want to be here alone."

What the son does not realize is that the father knows the son loves him; the father has already forgiven the son. The father sings, "You might say that it's over; you might say you don't need me, you don't miss me, but I know that you do."

Both father and son know that "love takes time" and forgiveness.

It isn't easy to forgive or to ask for forgiveness. Love does take time to heal the relationships in our life. The most important thing of all is never to forget the Father's love and never-ending forgiveness for each one of us.

"Pray," by M.C. Hammer: "Pray," a lively rap, is an unusual anthem to the power of prayer—"We've got to pray just to make it today."

The song talks about prayer being important even when things go well and how it should be a regular part of our life: "On my knees every night, you know I pray."

Sometimes we feel like we are going nowhere. "Time and time and time and time again . . . I kept on knocking, but nothing happens until I pray." This reminds us of Jesus' words to us: "'Ask, and you will receive; seek, and you will find; knock, and the door will be opened to you'" (see Matt. 7:7–11).

The song closes with a reminder that we should dedicate all we do to the glory of God: "We're sending this one out to the Lord . . . and we want to say thank you to the Lord with all our love."

"And So It Goes," by Billy Joel: In everyone's life, the time comes when someone or something disappoints us. We can lose our faith in others and even in God.

It can be scary to trust another, especially when we have been hurt. But we need to remember that "in every heart there is a room, a sanctuary safe and strong to heal the wounds," and there we can find God.

Sometimes we think that no one else can possibly feel as we do, yet God knows. God is "the only one who knows."

God is always there for us, even when we feel like no one else is. God is always there . . . even when we are not aware of it.

(For a Gospel parallel to this theme, see Matt. 11:28–30.)

"Something to Believe In," by Poison: In today's world, we're all looking for "something to believe in." But we aren't the first to feel this way. Somehow, I can even imagine the Pharisees singing this song as they challenged Jesus.

So much around us can cause doubt: TV evangelists preaching for dollars, the threat of war, the seemingly senseless death of a friend, homeless people sleeping on the streets. It can make us wonder "why so many lose and so few win."

It is okay to search for the answers; that is part of our journey through life. But we need to learn to look to Jesus for the answers.

Even one of Jesus' own disciples doubted him once (see John 20:24–29). Like Thomas, we too might say to Jesus, "Give us something to believe in." Jesus showed Thomas and us how real the wounds of the cross were, but he also showed how real are his Resurrection and our salvation. He truly gives us "something to believe in."

"From a Distance," by Bette Midler: When I first heard "From a Distance," I didn't like it because I cannot imagine a God that watches us from a distance. I think of God as being with us and around us. But one teen told me how comforting it is for her to know that God is watching over us and keeping us safe.

It is true that from a distance the world seems beautiful and all seem to live in harmony. "There are no guns or hungry mouths to feed." But Jesus didn't look at life from a distance. He reached out to all in need, even the outcasts and sinners.

If we are to truly live as Christians, we cannot allow ourselves to look at injustice and poverty from a distance. We need to follow Jesus' example and make a difference in the world around us.

(For a Gospel parallel to this theme, see Luke 19:1–10.)

"I Wanna Be Rich," by Calloway: If ever there was a theme song for the commercialism and materialism of the eighties and nineties, "I Wanna Be Rich" is it.

In magazines, on television, and on billboards, we see and hear the familiar refrain "I want money, lots and lots of money. . . ."

Sometimes we don't even realize the power that commercialism and materialism have over us. We need the right kind of jeans to be cool, the right kind of look to be liked, the right kind of sneakers to be athletic, and the best software to be successful.

The story Jesus told of the rich fool (Luke 12:13–21) reminds us of what happens to people who live this song. The rich man spent all his life hoarding his wealth, and what did it gain him? His motto was "Take life easy, eat, drink, and enjoy yourself." But in death he had nothing, for he failed to be rich in God's sight.

"Love . . . Thy Will Be Done," by Martika: One of the toughest parts of the Lord's Prayer to live out is the one featured in the title of this song—"Thy will be done."

When we pray, we often ask God to do our will rather than ask to be able to accept God's will. The singer of this song talks about trying to run and hide from God's will but, after accepting it, finding a new "power to keep up the fight."

In a very secular world, it does take a lot of courage to "strive for the glorious and the divine." We are all searching for peace in our life and our world, and by making God's will our own, "even when there's no peace outside my window, there's peace inside."

The next time you pray the Lord's Prayer, think about what you really mean when you say, "Thy will be done." Take time to pray and ask God's help to discern what God wants for your life. Learn to pray, "Your will be mine."

(For a Gospel parallel to this theme, see Matt. 6:5–15.)

"Hole Hearted," by Extreme: The singer of "Hole Hearted" is searching for inner peace but may have tried to fill that emptiness with all the wrong things. Perhaps he is thinking about God when he says, "There's a hole in my heart that can only be filled by you; and this hole in my heart can't be filled with the things that I do."

The singer laments, "If I'm not blind, why can't I see?" Spiritual blindness can be devastating. Perhaps that is why, in the Gospels, Jesus says that the faith of the blind man was what actually restored his sight (Luke 18:35–43). Jesus wanted him to be able to see with his heart and with the eyes of faith.

Many of us too have a "heart of stone," where we hide, yet we do not need to be afraid, because God promises to take our heart of stone and turn it into a heart of flesh (Ezek. 36:24–28).

Take some time to examine your conscience and those things that you keep in your heart of stone. What do you need in order to go from being "hole hearted" to being "whole hearted"?

"Winds of Change," by Scorpions: We are living in exciting times. The last few years have seen incredible changes in the world community. The song "Winds of Change" asks the former Soviet people, "Did you ever think that we could be so close, like brothers?"

The rapid changes around the world remind us of when Jesus told the Apostles, amazed at his teaching, that anything is possible with God (Mark 10:27).

The title of the song recalls how the Holy Spirit first came to the Apostles in the form of wind and fire (Acts 2:1–13). The Apostles listened to the "winds of change" and were able to go out and spread the message of Jesus Christ.

"The future is in the air, we can feel it anywhere." The Holy Spirit is like our breath of fresh air. We need to be open to the Holy Spirit working in our everyday life and in the events of the world. Are you open to what the Spirit is calling you to do?

Together we can create a better world "where the children of tomorrow share their dreams with you and me."

"Place in This World," by Michael W. Smith: "Place in This World" could easily become an anthem for all of us, especially teens who are searching for their "place in this world."

Have you ever asked the question, "Where do I belong?" Sometimes we wonder how God can hear us pray, when there are "millions on their knees." We can feel "the wind moving," we know the Holy Spirit is with us, yet we often "feel like we're standing still."

"This becoming is harder than it seems," yet we are not alone in our search for meaning. The singer of "Place in This World" realizes that when "there's not a lot to lean on," he needs the light of Christ to help him find his "place in this world."

Jesus says, "'I am the light of the world'" (John 8:12). When we feel lost, we need only look to Jesus to be our light in the darkness. Jesus shines through the people in our life who offer support and encouragement.

It is important to keep "a heart that's hopeful, a head that's full of dreams," but we can't forget to make Jesus a part of our life. Only then can we truly find our "place in this world."

Prayer Service "From Sin to Salvation"

Featuring the Use of Music

In addition to music, other prayer forms found in this prayer service are drama, scriptural prayer, and quiet prayer.

Themes found in this prayer service are pride, judging others, materialism, parent-teen relationships, boy-girl relationships, reconciliation and forgiveness.

Supplies

Recordings of three or four contemporary songs with negative messages, a tape player or CD player, a Bible, paper, a pen or a typewriter

Preparation

Ask the teens to find several contemporary songs with negative messages and to identify the sinful behavior or idea found in each one. Choose three or four of the songs, with differing messages, and divide the teens into small groups—one group for each song you've chosen. Ask each group to do the following:
- write a two-minute dialog from their own experience to match the tone of the song
- write ten to twelve questions for an examination of conscience that will challenge young people to look at their own behavior and prepare for the sacrament of reconciliation

Ask the teens to choose readers for the segments of dialog and examinations of conscience. Give the teens time to practice the dialog so it can be spoken rather than read.

Ask a teen to prepare to do the scriptural reading.

Write or type out the order of prayer, to be photocopied and distributed to the teens.

Procedure

Note: The songs, segments of dialog, and examinations of conscience offered here are examples of what your teens might come up with in the preparation step. Substitute your teens' ideas for these examples to make the service "theirs."

Call to prayer: Distribute the order of prayer to the teens.

Song: "I'm Too Sexy," by Right Said Fred

Dialog

> *First:* Did you see what he is wearing?
>
> *Second:* Yeah, he must be a real jerk.
>
> [*Pause.*]
>
> *First:* Oh, I just have to have a pair of earrings like that.
>
> *Second:* But you don't have the money.
>
> *First:* Well, I'll find some way to get it.
>
> [*Pause.*]
>
> *First:* Did you hear what they are saying about Karen?
>
> *Second:* Do you think she really did it?
>
> *First:* Wait until I tell Arlene.

Examination of conscience

- Do I think only of myself?
- Do I place too much value on appearance?
- Do I judge others by the clothes they wear?
- Do I step on others to get what I want?
- Do I hurt the feelings of others with my words or actions?
- Do I place myself above others?
- Do I flaunt my physical features?
- Do I talk only about myself all the time?
- Do I have an ego so big that there is no room for God?

Song: "No Son of Mine," by Genesis

Dialog

> *Father:* Do you know what time it is?
>
> *Son:* Yeah, so?
>
> *Father:* Come back here. I'm talking to you.

Son: What do you want?

Father: I asked you to be home at midnight. Don't you ever listen?

Son: I'm sick of living with all these stupid rules. I can't wait until I can move out!

Examination of conscience

- Have I disobeyed my parents?
- Have I spoken to them in a disrespectful tone?
- Have I tuned them out when they were talking to me?
- Have I failed to pull my fair share at home?
- When have I been rude to my brothers and sisters?
- When have I really hurt my family with my words or actions?
- When have I embarrassed my family by my behavior outside of home?

Song: "Passion," by Rhythm Syndicate

Dialog

First: How is it going with your girlfriend?

Second: Okay, I guess.

First: Have you gone to bed with her yet?

Second: No, not yet.

First: Why not? What is wrong with you?

Second: I'm looking for an opportunity.

First: You're going to be the last virgin in this high school.

Examination of conscience

- Have I used suggestive or vulgar language?
- Have I ever treated someone like a warm body instead of like a real person who deserves respect?
- Have I ever talked about members of the other sex in a way that demeans them?
- Do I allow myself to get into situations where I might not be able to control myself?
- Do I watch movies or listen to songs that glamorize sin?

Reading: Matt. 11:28–30 ("'Come to me . . .'")

Directions for individual reconciliation: Give appropriate directions for individual reconciliation.

Closure: Close the prayer service with quiet time and allow the participants to leave whenever they are ready to do so.

3
Scriptural Prayer:
Looking at the Scriptures with a New Lens

Overview One of my best experiences with the Scriptures and prayer occurred during a liturgy at a youth ministers' retreat. After the Gospel was proclaimed, we gathered in groups of four or five and took turns sharing what the passage said to us. It helped me realize that the Scriptures are not just something proclaimed *at* us or that happen *to* us, but we need to *break them open* and *climb inside* to discover what they mean to us.

Many of the young people we encounter are not familiar with the Scriptures. They may not attend Mass regularly to hear the Scriptures read in the liturgy of the word. Many do not own a Bible. Consequently, encouraging them to participate in the Mass and finding a way to get a Bible in their hands is worth a try. When I graduated from eighth grade, my teacher gave each student a copy of the Good News New Testament. I cannot say I read it much at that time, but over the years it became like an old friend, always there to come home to. Every time I look at that Bible, a bit yellow and worn now, I think of the invitation Sister Joan gave me.

Before we can convince teens to fall in love with the written word of God, we must first make the experience of listening to the Scriptures exciting and appealing. A way to do this is to weave the Scriptures into prayer and, in prayerful reflection, to draw parallels between the Scriptures and the teens' everyday life. After a while, whenever they hear the Scriptures or read them, they will make the connections themselves.

We also have to take a look at our own habits of reading the Bible. Don't tell teens to read the Bible if you don't read it yourself. If reading the Bible is at the end of our list of things to do, how can we expect teens to get excited about making it a priority in their life?

Only in the reading, and rereading, of a passage do we begin to find the insights contained in it. Consider doing this kind of praying over a passage yourself before using it with the teens. In discovering the deeper meanings, in looking at the Scriptures with a new lens, you will become better able to help the teens discover meaning for themselves.

The Scriptures can

• offer new and exciting insights into everyday experiences every time they are read
• invite teens to a closer relationship with Jesus through experiencing the stories of his life and teachings
• enable teens to find the roots of their faith and the Catholic religion
• give teens concrete examples of how to live their faith
• offer strength to deal with tough times and a means to celebrate the joys in life

Recently, a fellow retreat coordinator and I began taking time to pray the liturgy of the word whenever we were at the retreat center together. It was really quite a simple thing to do, but we were astounded by the way the Holy Spirit spoke to our ministry by way of the scriptural readings. It also gave a special boost of energy to our work with the teens, especially during the hectic season of Lent.

Guidelines

1. Approach the Scriptures with excitement and anticipation. Your attitude will be contagious.
2. Make the Scriptures readily accessible to the teens. Place some Bibles in the chapel or prayer space. Help the teens purchase a Bible if they do not have their own. Encourage them to read the Scriptures on their own.
3. Avoid telling the teens what a scriptural passage means. Instead, invite them to explore the personal meaning, like you have done. Honor the diversity of their reflections.
4. Encourage both individual and group prayer with the Scriptures.
5. Help the teens imagine the scene that is taking place in the passage they are reading, and help them look for the symbols the scriptural writer uses.
6. Help the teens connect the meanings they discover in the Scriptures with everyday living. Challenge them to connect insight and action.
7. Get the teens involved in reading and proclaiming the Scriptures in the Mass and in prayer services.

8. Remember that there are two parts to the Scriptures. Help teens enjoy the richness of the Hebrew Scriptures as well as the Christian Testament and become comfortable with them. The Psalms can be especially appealing to teens.

9. Go beyond the most familiar scriptural passages and introduce the teens to other books of the Bible.

10. Be conscious of inclusive language. Do not be afraid to adjust passages that come across as sexist or demeaning.

11. Allow time for the teens to reflect on and prepare for a passage before they are to read it during liturgy.

12. Show the teens that the Scriptures were not just written "by some old dudes"—that every time we read or experience them, we rewrite them with our own life.

Prayer Starters

Here are some possibilities for incorporating the Scriptures into prayer experiences:

Using the Scriptures in General

1. Write several different scriptural passages separately on large cards. Scatter the cards on a table in the center of the prayer space. Allow the teens to choose the passage they would like to read during the prayer service.

2. Rewrite a parable in a contemporary setting, perhaps in the town where most of the teens live or in the classroom of the school that many of them attend.

3. Divide a lengthy scriptural passage into several segments, each segment to be read by a different teen.

4. Place an open Bible in your prayer space and give the teens a written invitation from Jesus to come and read the Scriptures anytime they like.

5. Give each of the teens a Bible and encourage them to find the passage that most relates to their life right now. During shared prayer, offer the teens the option to read a few verses and share the meaning the passage has for them.

6. Expose the teens to passages as they are found in different versions of the Bible. If a retreat theme focuses on a particular passage, read the different versions of the passage at different times during the retreat.

7. Give the teens access to a variety of craft and art supplies and allow them time to illustrate a scriptural passage in the medium they are most comfortable with.

8. Send the teens on a "double scriptural scavenger hunt." Give them clues to find hidden cards that cite scriptural passages. When they find a card, they are to look up the cited passage, read it, and note what it says. The cards also give clues to the location of further cards . . . and the hunt goes on.

9. Give each of the teens a prayer journal as a gift at the beginning of Lent or Advent. Prepare the journals by writing a scriptural passage at the top of each page. Encourage the teens to read a passage a day during the season and to write a few lines of their reflection.

10. Center each witness talk at a retreat around a teaching of Jesus found in the Scriptures, with an invitation to follow his example in our own lives.

11. Find an article in the newspaper that has a parallel with a scriptural passage. Read both the article and the passage and pray about them with the group.

12. Referring to a parable that involves several characters, invite the teens to pray as the character they most relate to in their life right now. For example, with the parable of the prodigal son, a teen would pray as the prodigal son if feeling in need of forgiveness, as the father if feeling the need to forgive someone, or as the older brother if feeling the need to be more accepting.

13. Rewrite a psalm in today's language. How would it sound in rap?

14. Invite the teens to add themselves to a scriptural story. What would they have done, or how would they have reacted, if they had been there?

15. After a retreat that centers around exploring the Scriptures, invite the teens to present a symbol of their favorite passage. Make the symbols a part of the offertory procession at a liturgy.

16. Ask the teens to write a prayerful response to a passage in which Jesus offers a specific challenge—for example, Jesus' encounter with the rich man (Mark 10:17–27).

Using Specific Scriptural Passages

Matt. 13:24–30: Take your group out into a parish or neighborhood garden for springtime weeding. After all the weeds are pulled, read the parable of the weeds. Reflect on the need to rid ourselves of sin before we are able to grow again in our relationship with God. End this time of prayer by planting some flowers in the garden for the entire parish or neighborhood to enjoy.

Mark 12:30: Make each part of Mark's passage about the great commandment a part of a prayer service:

Read, "'Love the Lord your God with all your heart,'" and have the young people write words of love on paper hearts.

Read, "'Love the Lord your God . . . with all your soul,'" and pause for silent reflection.

Read, "'Love the Lord your God . . . with all your mind,'" and ask the teens to think of ways God's word has touched them.

Read, "'Love the Lord your God . . . with all your strength,'" and lead an activity in which the entire group must support each other physically.

Luke 9:18–20: Ask the teens to take some quiet time to answer Jesus' question "'Who do you say I am?'" Have them share responses during shared prayer.

John 19:31–37: Use the passage about the piercing of Jesus' side in a penance service:

Show the scene from the movie *Jesus of Nazareth* in which Jesus is crucified. Allow time for silence.

Lead the teens in an examination of conscience.

Read the scriptural passage and allow time for the teens to receive the sacrament of reconciliation.

2 Cor. 4:7–10: Invite a potter to come to your prayer space and set up a wheel and make pottery. Invite the teens to watch and ask questions. Call the teens to prayer while the potter continues working quietly.

Read 2 Cor. 4:7–10. Give each of the teens a small clay gardening pot as a symbol of themselves, and suggest that they write a prayer asking God to come and dwell in them.

Phil. 3:12–14: Run a few laps with the teens before reading Paul's passage about running toward the goal. Take time to reflect on the things that really are important in life. For example, If God isn't my God, what am I running toward? End your run at a shrine, a church, or another sacred space familiar to the teens.

James 2:14–18: Use James's passage about faith and action as a springboard for a commissioning service for peer leaders or peer helpers.

Create a banner with a large arrow in the middle pointing to the right. Invite the teens to write faith ideas such as feeding the hungry on the left side and concrete strategies for putting faith into action on the right side.

Exod. 20:1–17: Turn Moses into a rap master and retell the entire story of the Ten Commandments in rap. Devote a verse of rap to each commandment, placing extra emphasis on how to follow the Commandments in today's society.

Isa. 49:15: Pair the reading of Isa. 49:15 with the song "Isaiah 49," by Carey Landry, and the Irish Blessing. Both talk about how "God holds us in the palm of his hand."

Create a large poster of a hand. Ask each person to place a photo of themselves in "God's giant palm" as a sign of their willingness to place themselves in God's hands and try to do God's will.

Ps. 92:1–4: Ask each person to bring some sort of musical instrument to prayer. It can be a traditional one, like a guitar or a flute; one used for fun, like a kazoo; or one that is "handmade," such as a comb or a cooking kettle with forks and knives for drumsticks.

Working together, play a song in praise of God. It can be taken from a songbook ("Like Cedars They Shall Stand," by Dan Schutte, is based on Psalm 92) or be of your own creation. Get everyone involved.

Prayer Service "Letting Grow in Love"

Featuring the Use of Scriptural Prayer

In addition to scriptural prayer, other prayer forms found in this prayer service are shared prayer, symbols, and creative prayer.

Themes found in this prayer service are faith, planting the seeds of faith, sharing the word of God, and Jesus as the true vine.

Supplies

A seed catalog, scissors, a pen, six Bibles, seed packets, a basket, assorted gardening supplies and equipment

Preparation

Make bookmarks for each of the service's six readings by cutting out a picture from a seed catalog and writing the citation on it. Place each one in a Bible to mark the place for the reader. Ask six teens to prepare to do the readings.

Buy enough seed packets for each participant. Try to get marigolds or other spring flowers. Place the seed packets in a basket for use in the affirmation exercise that closes the service.

Collect a variety of gardening supplies and equipment. Examples of items are a shovel, a trowel, a spade, gardening gloves, a watering can, potting soil, a seed starter kit, a packet of seeds, a flowerpot, plant markers, pruning shears, a plant stake, a plant light, and a kneeler pad. You might ask each young person to bring a gardening item with them to prayer to arouse their curiosity and provide a larger variety to choose from for shared prayer. Arrange the items in the center of the prayer space, where they can easily be seen by all.

Procedure

Call to prayer: Tell the young people something along the following lines:

> During our time together, we have all grown in some way. We are not exactly the same people who came here a short while ago. For many of us, seeds have been planted that will not bear fruit right away. For others of us, the growth may be rapid and surprising.
>
> Each of us plays a critical part in allowing the word of God to grow within us. We gather now to ask God's help to grow in faith beyond this time together and throughout our lives.

First reading: Matt. 13:1–9 (the parable of the sower)

Prayers for growth: After the first reading and each of the following readings, invite the teens to come to the center of the prayer space one at a time, select one of the symbols from among the gardening supplies, and say a prayer that related to the seed theme and the symbol they are holding.

The following are examples of prayers that relate to the seed theme and a few of the gardening supplies.
- Lord, help me to dig deep within myself to find the courage to follow you. [Spade]
- Lord, help me to create a fertile place in my heart where your word can take root and grow. [Seed starter kit]
- Lord, help me to prune away all the people and things that keep me from embracing your love for me. [Pruning shears]

After four or five young people have held a symbol and said a prayer, move on to the next reading and repeat the ritual.

Note: As a variation to this sequence, you might share the first three readings, break once in the middle of the service for all the teens to share their prayers for growth, and then continue with the last three readings.

Second reading: Mark 4:30–32 (the parable of the mustard seed)

Prayers for growth

Third reading: Matt. 13:24–30 (the parable of the weeds)

Prayers for growth

Fourth reading: Matt. 24:32–35 (the fig tree)

Prayers for growth

Fifth reading: Luke 6:43–44 (a tree and its fruit)

Prayers for growth

Sixth reading: John 15:1–4 (Jesus, the real vine)

Closure: As a closure to the prayer service, conduct an affirmation exercise, telling the group the following:

> Jesus is the vine, and we are the branches. As we leave here, we remember that we must support and encourage each other. We must be Christlike for each other. We must be the ones to bring others to the Lord.

Take a packet of seeds, give it to a teen along with a hug, and say, "May God help your faith to grow." Then invite all to respond, "Amen."

Have each person, one at a time, repeat the above ritual for the person next to her or him, and so on, until everyone has been affirmed.

4
Shared Prayer:
Fun Ways to Pray Aloud

Overview

I remember browsing through a book on prayer and being struck by the illustration at the start of the chapter on shared prayer. The drawing was of a man with his hair standing straight up, looking like he had seen a ghost.

Teens and adult leaders often have that same response when anticipating shared prayer. Shared prayer can be seen as scary and something to avoid. Yet some of the most beautiful prayer experiences I have ever had with teens were in the context of shared prayer.

One of the retreats I have developed includes a prayer service in which we use Christmas lights for a shared prayer on the theme of thanksgiving. One by one, the teens offer a prayer of thanksgiving for someone who has been the light of Christ in their life. They then gently place a light bulb into a socket on a chain of lights that has been shaped like a cross on the floor of the prayer space. After the prayers are finished, we light the string of lights and pray the Lord's Prayer together.

If some of the lights do not light at first, the young people move quickly to work with the bulbs until they all light up. In that little twist in the ritual, we learn that sometimes we all need a little help in order to shine for Christ.

Once, when the sharing of prayers was finished, a seasoned youth minister who had participated took me aside and said, "I was amazed at the spirituality of these teens. I didn't think they had it in them."

Shared prayer can

- help young people realize that prayer can be both a personal and a communal experience
- give teens a stronger link to the faith community
- be a personal support for those who pray
- give teens a safe and comfortable way to witness to what they believe
- draw on the support of the faith community to pray for a special request or intention

While you may not need a lot of supplies for this form of prayer, it is important to spend extra time preparing. The most important ingredient is that the teens feel comfortable, both with the environment and with the other persons they will be praying with. Make sure your group knows what to expect and has time to prepare.

You take some risks with shared prayer. There may be times when no one accepts the invitation to pray and other times when prayer goes on longer than expected. The degree of response is often impossible to predict.

I remember working a retreat with a group of ninth graders who were particularly rowdy. I was exhausted by the time we got to night prayer and was sure that the silliness I had experienced all day would carry into the shared prayer I had planned. I even thought about skipping shared prayer in favor of a briefer, more controlled form of prayer. The faster I could get the kids to bed, the better.

After offering the invitation to shared prayer, I realized with a start that the class clown was sitting next to the person on my left. He would be one of the first to pray. I was sure the silence we had managed to gain would degenerate quickly into chaotic laughter, and the mood would be broken.

I held my breath as the candle was passed to him. But the prayer he shared came right from his heart: "Dear God, please help people to look beyond the crazy face I wear all the time and see the real me. I know I don't always take you seriously, but I really do want to be closer to you."

Guidelines

1. Make the setting comfortable.
2. Allow enough time for the participants to think, reflect, and compose a prayer before asking them to share their prayer.
3. Keep the directions simple; don't ask for too much.
4. When asking the teens to write their own prayer, let them know ahead of time if they will be invited to share it out loud.
5. Never force a teen to pray out loud; always provide an easy way to pass.

6. Use shared prayer after the young people have had a chance to get acquainted—for example, on the last day of a retreat weekend or well into the school year.
7. Use peer pressure in a positive way. Ask the teen leaders of your group to begin shared prayer in order to give the other teens an idea of the type or style of prayer to offer.
8. Do not be discouraged if your first attempts at shared prayer are met with silence. Offer the invitation and wait. Then try again. Teens will join in when they are ready.
9. Vary your approach to shared prayer. The teens will get bored if you do it the same way every time.
10. Use this type of prayer sparingly and in combination with other styles of prayer. Alternate the options of praying orally or in writing.

Sometimes the results of shared prayer are treasures to reflect on for a long time. An example that is dear to me is the "Creed for Life" written by teens on the first pro-life weekend retreat held in my diocese.

Near the end of the retreat, small groups of teens were asked to write and share a few statements of belief about being pro-life. They later put these together in a creed that they read together at a concluding service. Each teen took home a copy of the creed, and it was later published in our diocesan newspaper so others could share in the prayer for life.

Creed for Life

We believe in life,
    all life,
        and every aspect of life.
We believe
    all life is precious, whether born or unborn.
    Life should be cherished and not taken away.
    Jesus calls us to speak for the silent ones.
    All life is vital, no matter how insignificant it may seem.
    A person's capabilities or incapabilities do not lessen their value in the eyes and heart of God.
    Pro-life is not just a fact; it is a state of mind, which we live every day.
    God created us for a purpose.
    We should take advantage of what life gives us and live life to the fullest.
    Children are the future; we are the future, and we can make a difference.
We believe that faith in God
    gives meaning and purpose
        to human life.

Prayer Starters

Shared Prayer in the Spoken Word

1. Ask each teen to write a petition on a slip of paper. Then collect the petitions in a bag. Pass the bag around the prayer circle, asking each person to pull out a petition and read it to the group.

2. Invite the teens to write and read the prayer of the faithful for parish Mass on a weekend.

3. Light one large pillar candle and turn off all the lights in the prayer space. Pass the candle around the group, asking the teens, as they hold the candle, to offer a prayer to Jesus and thank him for lighting up their life.

4. Put a "prayer chair" in the center of your gathering. Whoever wants to start or continue shared prayer can do so from the chair.

5. Invite the teens to go for a walk in a nearby park. Ask them each to bring back something that moves them to prayer—but to be sure to do this without harming the environment. They can share the items from their walk during a prayer service on preserving the gifts of nature.

6. During a prayer service on sharing light with others, form a circle and give each person a taper candle. Have one person complete the phrase "My special light is . . ." and then light the candle of the next person, and so on, continuing the light and the prayer around the circle.

7. Pass a real red rose around the prayer circle and ask each person to say a prayer for someone who is "life endangered"—the unborn, people with AIDS, or the elderly.

8. Ask the teens to volunteer to teach basic prayers, such as the Lord's Prayer and the Hail Mary, to young children in the parish school or religious education program.

9. Pick up one of those red "stress dolls" that allow you to squash the head, which always bounces back to its original shape. Pass the doll around the prayer circle and offer prayers for the ability to get through stressful times.

10. Invite an older teen to give a witness talk about how tough it is to pray sometimes, but how important prayer has become in her or his life.

11. Initiate a discussion on the many ways we address God when we pray. Affirm each person's choice to pray in the way he or she is most comfortable. Create a poster with a collage of the many names for God and hang it up in your prayer space.

12. During a weekly teen prayer gathering, invite the participants to read their favorite scriptural passage and share the meaning found there for them.

13. Encourage the teens to pray for each other on a regular basis: for help on a test, for success in a track meet, for a safe ride home, in thanksgiving for a job well done, and so forth.

14. Help the teens deal with the death of a classmate by giving them a comfortable place to grieve with each other and a chance to thank God for the gift of the person who died.

15. During an agape prayer service, ask the teens to share bread together and, as they do so, to say, "Thank you for being bread for me."

16. Encourage the teens to attend a parish RCIA class and to join in the prayer. The teens could pray for the candidates, and the candidates could pray for the teens.

17. During a prayer service, ask the teens to break into small groups to reflect on the meaning of a scriptural reading before continuing the service.

Shared Prayer in the Written Word

1. Buy a large book with ruled pages and keep it in a special place in your school chapel or group gathering place. Invite the teens to write down their prayer intentions anytime. Ask the entire community to remember these intentions in their prayers.

2. At the start of a weekend retreat, put a prayer box (a shoe box is fine) for each retreatant in a readily accessible place. During the retreat, ask the teens to write a prayer for each person and put it in that person's box. The retreatants can then take their box home and read a prayer a day until all are gone.

3. During Advent, find out the needs of a local shelter for pregnant teens or homeless women. Decorate a parish Christmas tree with paper ornaments that indicate a need on one side and a prayer intention on the other. Ask parishioners to take an ornament, donate a gift, and offer the prayer.

4. When working with a large group, ask the group members to write prayers of petition on slips of paper. Collect the prayers in baskets during the offertory portion of a Mass and place them near the altar.

5. Ask the members of your group to write original prayers for their parents. Print the prayers in small booklets to give as gifts for Mother's Day and Father's Day.

6. As a Lenten project, arrange for the young people to make a prayer book for shut-ins to read each day of Lent. Include both traditional and original prayers.

7. As a service project, help your teens plan and serve a Communion breakfast for the members of the parish. Decorate special placemats with original prayers for the diners to read during the meal and take home with them.

8. Write postcard prayers to send to shut-ins so they get a prayer in the mail at least once a month.

Prayer Service "Letting the Leaves Fall"

Featuring the Use of Shared Prayer

In addition to shared prayer, other prayer forms found in this prayer service are symbols, prayer in a different setting, creative prayer, storytelling, and scriptural prayer.

Themes found in this prayer service are transitions, changing relationships, God's gift of the seasons, hope, the need for God, and individuality.

Supplies

A lawn or field full of leaves; a Bible; a copy of "The Last Leaf," by
O. Henry; index cards; a pen or a typewriter; waxed paper; an iron

Preparation

Since this prayer service is seasonal, make sure that you have access to
an area with a large amount of leaves and that the service is held at a
time of day when it will be light outside. You may want the teens to
gather in an indoor prayer space following the leaf search, or if weather
permits, you may want to hold the entire prayer service outside.

Note: If you want to use this prayer service outside of the fall season,
consider using symbols other than fall leaves. Use symbols consistent
with the season.

Ask one teen to prepare to do the scriptural reading and one teen
to prepare to read the story by O. Henry (the first and second readings,
respectively).

Prepare cards with the response that all will read together after
the second reading.

Procedure

Call to prayer: Introduce the prayer service in the following way:

> Look around you at the leaves still clinging to the trees and the
> ones surrounding you on the ground. Take notice of the variety of
> colors and the many different shapes and sizes of the leaves.
>
> Fall is a spectacular season. It reminds us that summer
> cannot continue forever, even though we may want it to, and that
> winter is part of each of our lives. Fall also reminds us that we too
> go through many changes in our life, make many transitions in
> our relationships, and face many challenges.

Leaf search: Ask the teens to walk around the area and try to find the
one leaf that they believe best represents themselves. (You may want to
choose your own ahead of time so you can give the teens an example.
In the past, I chose a leaf that was fiery red and bright yellow, because I
am angry sometimes and cheerful other times. The leaf was a little dry
on the edges, because sometimes I get discouraged, but it had a green
stem that reminded me that I am still connected to God by my faith.)

Ask the teens to gather together in the prayer space as soon as
everyone has found their leaf. Then continue with the prayer service.

First reading: Eccles. 3:1–8 (a time for everything)

Variation: Consider doing a mime of the passage from Ecclesiastes.

Shared prayer: Ask the teens, one at a time, to show the rest the leaf
they chose and how it represents themselves.

Second reading: "The Last Leaf," by O. Henry

Response: Ask all to read the following prayer:

Dear God,
We can see the beautiful things in this world.
We can hear the drumming of the rain and feel the gentle breezes.
But, God, make us more sensitive to the beauty.
Let us see the extraordinary in the ordinary.
Grant that our eyes may see the colors, whether vibrant or faint, more clearly for what they are.
May our ears listen to your symphony of sounds more intently and the slightest sensations fill every part of us.
May the fragile scent of the rose smell sweeter each time it is encountered and the magnificent details of the earth not be overlooked.

[Adapted from the original by Sheri Harrison]

Closure: Close the prayer service by asking the teens to set their prayer leaf aside and join in a joyous romp in the leaves.

After the prayer service, suggest to the young people that they preserve and treasure their prayer leaf by iron-pressing it between two pieces of waxed paper.

5
Drama, Dance, and Mime: Giving Movement to Prayer

Overview

When I was starting out in retreat ministry, just a few months out of college and ready to say yes to anything, I was asked to do some clown ministry for a freshman-sophomore retreat program called "Sunrise."

My character's name was Person, and I made several appearances throughout the retreat: to act out a scriptural passage, to lead the group in prayer, to add hand motions to the Lord's Prayer, and to give love away in the form of red felt hearts.

To say I was reluctant at first would be an understatement. I could not believe I had agreed to do this. But as the makeup went on, my inhibitions came off. I discovered a gift I had never known I had and a way to reach teens that I will always cherish.

I stopped being Maryann and became Person. Maryann was shy and kind of clumsy, but Person was agile and confident, sensitive and graceful. In the role of Mary Magdalene asking Jesus for forgiveness, I cried real tears for Mary, myself, and the teens.

In these prayer experiences I found a powerful way to reach the teens and a way to deepen my own spirituality—all through the eyes of a clown.

Drama, dance, and mime can

- challenge teens to use gifts and talents they never knew they had
- catch and hold the attention of teens with a powerful invitation to active worship
- get teens out of their routines and give new expression to their prayer
- tap the musical and dramatic talents of teens to share their gifts with each other and the wider community
- reawaken a sense of childhood imagination, wonder, and creativity often forgotten, and get teens excited about preparing for prayer
- share the Gospel message with children of all ages
- use humor, laughter, and grace to get a message to those who are difficult to reach

The arts are a great way to reach small and large groups, to build community and allow teens to enjoy a sense of accomplishment. Drama, dance, and mime offer an exciting way to share the message of Jesus Christ.

Prayer that includes such art forms can indeed have a powerful impact, but it is not a common part of parish ritual. While paintings and sculpture are readily acceptable, drama, dance, and mime are still experienced as strange by many in most parishes.

To include these forms of prayer in the wider parish or diocesan community may require a bit of convincing. During the first youth rally in our diocese, we planned to have a parish youth group perform a liturgical dance during the offertory procession at Mass. The master of ceremonies for the bishop sent back the outline of our plans for the liturgy with his reservations about the dancing.

On Youth Day, however, his fears were allayed. The teens had practiced for weeks, and they performed a most reverent dance in costumes made lovingly by their parents. Their dance did not detract from the liturgy as he feared, but drew all who were present more deeply into the liturgy of the Eucharist.

Guidelines

1. Never force anyone to take part in drama, dance, or mime. Encourage participation and the freedom of creative expression, but also allow the choice to watch.
2. Try to get everyone involved. Teens who feel uncomfortable acting or dancing can be recruited to write scripts, make costumes, or be stagehands for productions.
3. Encourage small-group work until the teens, either as individuals or as a group, are comfortable and confident enough to perform before an audience.
4. Give the young people adequate instruction and guidance in the art form that is to be used. Give them plenty of time to practice their presentations.
5. Insist that performers make a commitment to regular rehearsals so they are well prepared to perform before a larger group.
6. Make sure that the teens create props that are easy to see and manage without detracting from the drama they are presenting.

7. Consult with other members of the parish staff, especially the pastor, when planning to use drama, dance, or mime as part of a liturgical celebration.

8. If the message intended by a performance the teens have attended is not clear, allow time for them to process and discuss the experience.

Prayer Starters

1. Invite the teens to write their own one-act plays that contain a lesson related to the challenge of living as a Christian in today's world.

2. Ask an adult leader to play the role of Jesus making an appearance on a modern-day talk show. The panelists or questioners could be youth group members.

3. Ask a teen to take the role of God and hide somewhere out of view, where he or she can be heard but not seen. "God" can challenge the other teens about the way they pray and whether they really mean the words they say.

4. Invite the teens to do a liturgical dance during the offertory procession at Mass, dressing the altar with the linens, candles, and flowers before bringing forth the gifts.

5. After the priest proclaims the Gospel at Mass, a group of teens could present a modern drama based on the reading. They could then work together with the priest in his homily to help the congregation connect the Gospel message with everyday life.

6. For the stations of the cross, invite teens to form a tableau for each station (that is, to depict a scene with the use of costumes while remaining silent and motionless).

7. Teach the teens the basics of mime and ask small groups to act out a parable in mime, using only themselves as props.

8. Ask the teens to add simple hand motions to one of their favorite hymns.

9. Challenge the teens to make their own "music video" for a contemporary song they plan to use during a prayer service.

10. Invite a community or college theater group to lead the teens in prayer at an annual youth day.

11. Introduce the teens to clown ministry and the concept of "being a fool for Christ," and how the gift of laughter and playfulness is a fun way to share the message of Jesus Christ.

12. Get the teens involved in helping parish children prepare a Nativity drama for presentation at a Christmas Mass or prayer service.

13. Put on a puppet show for the children of the parish, relating the theme of sacramental preparation.

14. On a visit to a nursing home, take along a puppet show or mime presentation on being a Christian.

15. Divide the teens into pairs and ask them to "mirror Christ" for each other: Without speaking, one person slowly makes a movement representing Jesus' words or actions. The second person mirrors the action, then adds her or his own. The first person mirrors that action, and the partners continue.

16. Combine sign language, liturgical dance, and mime for a prayer service in which the readings are signed, the songs have movement, and the responses are done in mime.

17. For a prayer service on "being yourself," ask each person to wear a costume over their clothing. While removing the costume as part of the service, each teen can pray, "Lord, I take off my mask of _____. Help me to _____."

18. As part of a prayer service on "following your conscience," stage an argument between the two sides of a person's conscience: one side urges the person to do something good, and the other gives persuasive arguments for making the wrong choice.

19. Bring two drama masks to the prayer circle—one comic and one tragic. Ask the teens to consider which mask they relate to when they approach prayer. Why? How would they like to change their attitude? What could they do to change it?

20. For a prayer service on parent-teen communication, ask the parents to take the role of the teens and the teens to take the role of the parents in short dramatizations of the many ways communication can break down.

21. Teach a group of teens how to do a choral reading of a scriptural passage. If they feel comfortable with the medium, lead them in creating their own choral reading of some favorite scriptural verse.

22. Act out excerpts from the popular musical plays *Jesus Christ Superstar* and *Godspell*.

23. In anticipation of the scriptural readings for the Palm Sunday liturgy, guide the teens in recreating the triumphant entry of Jesus into Jerusalem, by holding a procession in the streets of the neighborhood around the parish.

Prayer Service "Apple of God's Eye"

Featuring the Use of Drama

In addition to drama, other prayer forms found in this prayer service are symbols, creative prayer, quiet prayer, scriptural prayer, and shared prayer.

Themes found in this prayer service are uniqueness, discovering our purpose, learning to love ourselves, "Beauty is only skin deep," and God's unconditional love.

Supplies

Apples, a basket

Preparation

Make sure you have enough apples so that everyone attending the prayer service will have one. Purchase apples in a variety of shapes, sizes, and colors. Place the apples in a basket in the center of your prayer space.

Ask two teens to prepare to perform the three-part skit that is provided in the procedure section for this service. They should do so to the extent that they need only refer briefly to the script while doing the skit. Tell them to adapt the wording to fit their own style, but without losing the meaning of the dialog.

Select a reader, or readers, for the scriptural phrases specified for this service.

Procedure

Call to prayer: Invite each person to come forward and take an apple out of the basket in the center of the prayer space. Ask the teens to take a few moments to quietly and carefully examine their apple.

Reflection questions: Ask the group to reflect on the following questions:

- What is an apple for?
- Who created your apple?
- How did it grow?

Part 1 of the skit: Signal for the two previously chosen players to carry out the first part of the skit:

First: Hey, _____, want an apple?

Second: No thanks. Apples are boring.

First: Oh, no, they come in all colors—green, red, yellow.

Second: I'd rather have a candy bar.

First: Some are sweet, and some are tart.

Second: And some are rotten—rotten to the core.

First: They are shiny and round and fun to eat, or to give as a gift.

Second: Or to throw at someone who bugs you.

First: You can bob for apples or make an apple pie.

Second: Or throw one at someone.

First: They're good for you too, you know. "An apple a day keeps the doctor away."

Second: Give me a break!

First: Did you know that apples have messages too?

Second: No, but I'll bet you're going to tell me.

First: No two apples are exactly alike, even if they are the same color.

Second: Neither are two Doritos.

First: Yet inside they are very similar, just like you and me.

Second: You've got to be kidding.

First: Each of us is unique, but we have more in common than we realize.

Pause for quiet reflection

Scriptural phrases: Have the previously selected teen, or teens, slowly read the following phrases, with a pause after each one.

> "There are different kinds of spiritual gifts, but the same Spirit gives them. There are different ways of serving, but the same Lord is served" [1 Cor. 12:4–5].

> "'Love one another, just as I love you'" [John 15:12].

> "'Do this in memory of me'" [Luke 22:19].

Questions for reflection: Request that the teens, in groups of two or three, reflect on and respond to the following questions, or ask them to write responses to the reflection questions during quiet time.

- What purpose does God have for you?
- How open are you to the work God has planned for you?
- What is one thing you can do to fulfill that purpose?
- When are you going to start?

Part 2 of the skit

First: Hey, _____, did you know that you are the apple of God's eye?

Second: Oh no, not again.

First: If you look close enough, the apple can tell you about God's love.

Second: I was afraid of that.

First: Did you know that God made you in God's image and loves you just the way you are?

Second: Not me.

First: God made you beautiful on the outside, but what's inside is what really counts. There is more to an apple than just its skin.

Second: No one sees what's inside.

First: But that's the best part of us. At the core of each of us is our true self and our faith in God.

Second: Most people throw apple cores away.

First: In today's world, that is often true, but you don't have to throw them away.

Second: Maybe you're right.

First: It's scary, I know, if you pray and do things God's way, but who knows what you'll discover? Why, there is actually a promise from God in each and every apple.

Second: Where?

First: If you cut an apple in half, in just the right way, you'll find the star of Bethlehem and the promise of Christmas.

Second: Do you still have an apple to spare?

First: [*Tossing an apple across room to Second*] Sure, there are always plenty of apples to go around.

Quiet time: Pause and ask everyone to pray silently that God will fill them with love and fulfill a divine purpose in their life.

Part 3 of the skit

Second: Hey, _____, how did you learn so much about apples and God?

First: I'm not afraid to peel the skin away and look beneath the surface.

Closure: Direct the young people to do an apple affirmation: tell them to give an apple to another person and to say one way that that person is "the apple of God's eye."

6
Traditional Prayers:
Old Favorites with a New Twist

Overview Traditional prayers are often the most taken for granted of all forms of prayer, but they are a rich part of our heritage. For many people, these familiar prayers and rituals are the most visible signs of our Catholic identity.

Some of my fondest memories of childhood are saying my prayers at bedside with my parents and learning to say the Lord's Prayer and the Hail Mary in Polish and English. Since my namesake is the patron saint of Poland and my birth month is May, traditions associated with Mary were very special to me.

Because we learn so many of the traditional prayers early and recite them often, we can become like the fast-talking advertising man, going through the words without noticing them at all. But traditional prayers serve as a connection between generations, a tie to our history, and a link between our local parish church and the rest of Catholics worldwide.

Traditional prayers can

- connect teens with their Catholic roots and Catholic identity
- help bridge the gap between generations and forge a link between teens and the rest of the parish community
- provide a source of strength and comfort in tough times when it is difficult to pray from the heart
- be readily prayed together with other Catholics both inside and outside the parish or school community
- provide a starting point for creative and personal prayer by offering models, structure, and a means for addressing God

Traditional prayers often get a bum rap. We assume wrongly that they cannot be from the heart since we did not compose them ourselves and they are often memorized. But the meaning of memorizing is to know *by heart.* Traditional prayers do have an important place in our liturgy and prayer experiences.

Being a cradle Catholic, throughout my entire life I have prayed the Lord's Prayer at Mass and on other occasions. Yet I never realized the depth of its meaning and beauty until I planned a weekend retreat around the prayer.

We took the prayer line by line to try to appreciate its meaning for us today. We found how rich a prayer it is that Jesus taught us: in one prayer we can praise God, promise to do God's will, seek bread for our body and our spirit, ask for forgiveness and the ability to forgive, and ask for protection from evil.

Guidelines

1. Ask the teens to slow down when praying traditional prayers and to think about what the words mean as they say them.
2. Give the teens the opportunity to share, in writing or orally, what some traditional prayers mean to them.
3. We can no longer assume that everyone knows the words to traditional prayers, because more and more teens do not have any formal religious education. Provide copies of the words for those who need to refer to them. Take the time to teach traditional prayers.
4. Adapt and update traditional prayers, but do not change them so much from their original form that they are no longer recognizable.
5. Vary the way you use traditional prayers. Consider adding music, slides, and responses.
6. Consider the historical context and add this to the introduction of traditional prayers.
7. Overcome negative stereotypes of traditional prayers by finding creative ways to share the prayers and helping the teens find the link between the words and their everyday experience.
8. Encourage the teens to keep a journal of their favorite traditional prayers and to add ones that they learn from family and friends.

During one reconciliation service, I heard a buzz going through a group of teens preparing to go to confession. One teen looked particularly distressed, so I took him aside and asked what was wrong. "I want to go to confession, but I don't know the Act of Contrition." He was not alone in his concern. I assured the teens that they could indeed compose their own act of contrition, but after their insistence, I wrote the words on a card that was exchanged dutifully at the door of the reconciliation room as one teen went in and another came out.

Faced with an experience that was somewhat scary in itself, the teens found security in a prayer they could hold in their hand and pray without stumbling.

Prayer Starters

1. Pray the Lord's Prayer as a group, but stop after "Give us this day our daily bread." Bake bread from scratch together. Continue the prayer after the group has broken and shared the bread.
2. Add a dialog component to a traditional prayer. For example, pray the Hail Mary, but pause after each line to add a response that Mary might make as we address the prayer to her.
3. Create an entire retreat weekend around the Prayer of Saint Francis, starting each part of the retreat with a prayerful witness talk on a part of the prayer.
4. With your teens, spend time in prayerful reflection on some of the prayers and responses we make at Mass. What do we really mean when we say, "The Lord is with you." "And also with you." Do we live with each other as if we believe this?
5. Put together a reconciliation service around these words from Mass: "Lord I am not worthy to receive you, but only say the word and I shall be healed."
6. Instead of using a traditional prayer at the start or close of a service, try weaving it throughout the entire service. For example, use the Glory Be as a refrain or response at certain times in the service.
7. Have the teens write responses to a traditional prayer, so the recited prayer is mixed with personal prayer. One terrific way to do this is for the teens to write responses to the statements of belief in the Apostles' Creed.
8. Assign teens to find the history of prayers that are traditionally Catholic and to share the history and meaning, in the hope that this will lead the teens to use the prayers more often.
9. Our parents and grandparents spent much more time memorizing prayers in their youth than we did in ours. Ask the teens to interview family members to find out what prayers those individuals learned as youth. Urge the teens to write down and learn the ones that are new to them and to use the prayers.
10. Encourage teens to use traditional prayers as a way to pray together as an informal group—before a basketball game, on a bus trip, or before the curtain goes up on a school play.
11. When praying with a very large group, create a living rosary: Each person represents one of the beads and holds a candle, and everyone sits on the floor in the outline of a rosary. As the prayer is said for each "bead," the candle that person is holding is lit to help everyone keep track of where they are in their prayer.
12. Challenge the teens to learn one of the traditional Catholic prayers in another language. Use these foreign-language forms during a prayer service on world peace or international understanding.

13. As a group, learn and pray a prayer in sign language.
14. Take a hike with your teens and stop every quarter mile to pray one of the stations of the cross.
15. Ask several teens to each mime a part of the Lord's Prayer, freezing in place as they finish their part of the prayer. Consider sharing this at a parish liturgy one Sunday.
16. Ask the teens to add their own personal ending to the Lord's Prayer, and then use the endings when praying traditional prayer combined with personal prayer.
17. Give each teen a copy of the Act of Contrition. Tell them to use this as a starting point for writing their own act of contrition during preparation time before receiving the sacrament of reconciliation.
18. Introduce the teens to the liturgy of the hours, which is prayed by priests, religious, and many laypeople. Give the teens some historical background and use some excerpts from the liturgy of the hours as part of regular prayer in the classroom or youth group.
19. Obtain a copy of the Catholic *Book of Blessings*. Suggest that the teens choose and use one of the blessings that fits into their life right now.
20. Ask the teens to collect traditional ethnic prayers and blessings to share with others in the group and use in group prayer services.
21. Encourage teens to help elderly parishioners bring in baskets of Easter food for a traditional blessing on Holy Saturday if that is a custom in your parish.
22. Challenge the teens to do some research on their favorite saint and to teach each other some of the prayers that are directed to saints.
23. Before a parish Forty Hours Devotion, ask the teens to sign up for half-hour devotions before the Blessed Sacrament.
24. Pray the divine praises used in the benediction and invite the young people to add their own personal prayers of praise and thanksgiving to God.

Prayer Service "Praying with Mary"

Featuring the Use of Traditional Prayers

In addition to traditional prayers, other prayer forms found in this prayer service are music, symbols, and scriptural prayer.

Themes found in this prayer service are devotion to Mary, mother-daughter relationships, accepting God's will, understanding the Hail Mary, sharing love, and devotion to the rosary.

Note: This prayer service is designed for mother-daughter participation on Mother's Day.

Supplies

A Bible; the words and music to "Hail Mary: Gentle Woman," by Carey Landry; two vases; a statue of the Blessed Mother; nine blue votive candles; matches; a taper candle; paper; a pen or a typewriter

Preparation

Ask each mother-daughter pair to bring a single flower to the prayer service.

Ask the daughters to buy or handcraft a rosary as a special Mother's Day gift for their mother. They should bring the wrapped gift with them to the prayer service but keep it out of sight.

Ask one mother-daughter pair to prepare to do the scriptural readings and another pair to prepare to lead the group in a decade of the rosary.

Ask another mother-daughter pair to be the leaders of song and to teach the closing song if it is unfamiliar to the group.

Place two empty vases on either side of a statue of the Blessed Mother and place nine blue votive candles in a semicircle in front of the statue.

Put the Memorare and the Hail Mary, the latter with responses, on prayer sheets. Arrange for the mothers and daughters to enter the chapel or prayer space during the opening song and place their flowers in the vases next to the statue of the Blessed Mother.

Procedure

Call to prayer: Sing the opening song, "Immaculate Mary."

The Memorare: Invite everyone to pray the Memorare together:

> Remember, O most gracious Virgin Mary,
> that never was it known
> that anyone who fled to your protection,
> implored your help
> or sought your intercession,
> was left unaided.
> Inspired by this confidence,
> we fly unto you, O Virgin of virgins, our Mother.
> To you do we come,
> before you we stand, sinful and sorrowful.
> O Mother of the Word Incarnate,
> despise not our petitions,
> but in your mercy hear and answer us. Amen.

First reading: Luke 1:26–38 (An angel appears to Mary and announces the conception of Jesus.)

The Hail Mary: Invite everyone to pray the following responses to the parts of the Hail Mary:

> *Leader:* Hail Mary.
>
> *All:* We praise you, our dear Mother.
>
> *Leader:* Full of grace.
>
> *All:* Free from the sin of this world.
>
> *Leader:* The Lord is with you.

All: Teach us to find him here with us.

Leader: Blessed are you among women.

All: Teach us to be blessings for each other.

Leader: And blessed is the fruit of your womb, Jesus.

All: Your son, our brother and savior.

Leader: Holy Mary, mother of God.

All: Show us how to live lives of holiness.

Leader: Pray for us sinners now.

All: Hear us as we place our prayers before you.

Leader: And at the hour of our death.

All: Show us the way to heaven; reunite us with your son.

Leader: Amen.

All: Amen.

As each part of the prayer is said, light one of the blue votive candles that were placed in front of the statue of Mary.

Second reading: John 19:25–27 (Jesus, when dying on the cross, asks John to take care of Mary his mother.)

Gifts for the mothers: Invite the daughters to present their gift of a rosary to their mother as a special Mother's Day gift.

The rosary: Ask the previously chosen mother-daughter pair to lead the group in praying one decade of the rosary.

Closure: Request that all join in the closing song, "Hail Mary: Gentle Woman," by Carey Landry.

7
Creative Prayer: Unlocking the Imagination

Overview

"The next activity is very simple," I tell the confirmation candidates on retreat. "All you have to do is answer one simple question: What is service?" Then I leave it up to them to decide how to express their answer.

Their answers to that question have taken shape in posters, poems, newspaper articles, mime, hand puppetry, rap, debates between devils and angels, and various other creations.

One of my favorite answers took the form of a mobile made from two hangers, poster board, magazines, string, and a lot of imagination. Five shapes hung from the mobile—a head, an ear, a mouth, a heart, and a hand. The explanation that accompanied the mobile said, "We need our head to think of ways to help others, our ears to listen to others' needs, our voice to spread God's word, our heart to show love for others, and our hands to reach out to everyone who needs us."

Most forms of prayer with teens need to be structured and directed, but there should also be plenty of flexibility to allow the young people to give wings to their creative imagination.

Creative prayer can

- offer ways of praising and worshiping God that go beyond the written or spoken word
- excite and surprise teens into praying in a new way
- help teens discover and use hidden talents
- reawaken a sense of imagination often relegated to early childhood
- highlight prayer as an ongoing part of life and initiate a search for God in the ordinary and the everyday

Most teens enjoy a chance to be creative in prayer, whether this means using newspaper clippings and glue, construction paper and scissors, or clay and their hands. Often, teens who otherwise have difficulty expressing themselves in prayer really take off when they have a chance to create the way they pray.

Being creative in prayer may require a little encouragement at first. Many of us are reluctant to show others our creative efforts, and it is easy to say, "I can't draw," or "I'm not good with anything artsy." But once they are into it, young people are surprised—and excited—by their ability to express prayer through simple art forms.

Guidelines

1. Use your imagination.
2. Experiment with different media. Allow the teens to discover for themselves which materials give them the greatest freedom of expression.
3. Seize the moment. Be open to prayer experiences that just happen. Be willing to adjust your schedule when the teens take an initiative in prayer.
4. Be alert for creative prayer possibilities that occur in everyday experiences. Jot down ideas as they come to you, no matter how crazy they might seem.
5. Encourage the teens to share their creativity with each other.

Creative prayer that incorporates the element of surprise can really give some special impact to a message you want to share. At the start of a retreat on gifts and giving, I place a brightly wrapped box in the center of the gathering. I tell the teens that the box must go with us everywhere during our retreat day—from activity to discussion to lunch, and so forth. During the day, they become more and more curious to discover what is inside. At the end of the closing liturgy, they open the box to discover a heart-shaped balloon inscribed with the words "God's love: the greatest gift."

Prayer Starters

1. Have the young people design a banner that announces the coming of Easter. Divide the assembling of the banner design into several stages. Hang the blank banner up on Ash Wednesday and add to the banner each week during Lent, with the final design appearing on Easter Sunday.
2. Cover an entire table with all sorts of common, and uncommon, craft and art supplies. Ask the teens to choose any medium they like and create a "visual" prayer.

3. If your group has its own newsletter, include a regular feature on prayer and urge the teens to take turns contributing original prayers and prayer ideas.

4. Take a trip to an art museum. Start with exhibits that are clearly religious and ask the teens to identify prayers that the artists might be expressing. Later, move into the more abstract exhibits and do the same. Challenge the teens to use their own artistic talents to praise God.

5. Make prayer banners for each member of the First Communion class of the parish. Hang the banners in the church for the First Communion Mass and then present them to the children at a community celebration afterward.

6. Give each of the teens a pipe cleaner and allow them to shape it any way they want in order to describe their relationship with God at the moment.

7. Challenge your group to write a prayer in poetry form, with each person contributing a line or stanza to the whole.

8. Teach the teens how to write poetry in the Japanese haiku style (a form of poetry written in seventeen syllables, divided into three lines of five, seven, and five syllables, respectively). Encourage the teens to use this style of poetry to write a prayer about the gift of nature.

9. Combine the written word and origami (the Japanese art of paper folding) by writing prayers and learning how to fold them into shapes that match the themes of the prayers.

10. Compose a prayer entirely out of words the teens cut out of newspaper headlines.

11. Use pictures to make up prayers. Don't forget to provide keys so that others will be able to decipher the prayers.

12. Buy a few rolls of black-and-white film and challenge the teens to create a visual prayer entirely out of black-and-white photographs. If possible, allow the teens the opportunity to develop and print the photos themselves.

13. Ask the teens to look for the coincidences or small miracles that happen in their everyday life. Use the occurrences as a springboard for prayer.

14. Give each of the teens a Bible and tell them to open it to any page and create a prayer relating to their own life based on what they find there.

15. Invite an artist to bring an abstract painting or sculpture to a group meeting. Give the teens time to study it carefully and write a prayer inspired by the creation. Encourage them to share their insights with each other.

16. Show the teens a personal prayer banner created by making a collage of greeting cards treasured over the years. Suggest that they make one and hang it in their room at home as a reminder to pray for loved ones who sent the cards.

17. Have the teens create their own holy cards to share with family, friends, parishioners, and shut-ins.

18. Locate some of the more beautiful and varied stained-glass windows in the churches in your area. Plan a field trip to see them.

Also, visit someone who works with stained glass to learn more about the art form. If possible, arrange for your group to do a small stained-glass project.

19. Create a banner in the style of a patchwork quilt, with each "patch" representing a teen's favorite prayer. Hang it in the church foyer for all the parishioners to enjoy.

20. Take the teens on a field trip to a junkyard. Challenge them to recycle materials they find into an off-the-wall sculpture. Have them create a prayer about caring for the environment to go along with the sculpture.

21. Give your teens a chance to grow a vegetable garden. Have them prepare a prayer for each of the works of planting, tending, and harvesting.

22. Play catch with a few Koosh balls. Use the unusual texture, color, and shape of these toys to lead a prayer on individuality.

23. Offer the teens the chance to learn the art of calligraphy so they can make elegant prayer cards for themselves and others.

24. Create a prayer space in the place where you meet. Cover the walls of the space with white butcher paper. Make a wide variety of art supplies available and give the teens the freedom to create a visual prayer that covers the entire wall space.

25. Collect the small boxes that paper clips come in. Fill each of them with a different short prayer. Hide them all over the school or parish building, Easter egg style. Let the young people have fun hunting for the boxes and finding the prayer messages inside.

Prayer Service "Discovering Christ in Each Other"

Featuring the Use of Creative Prayer

In addition to creative prayer, other prayer forms found in this prayer service are symbols, music, scriptural prayer, and quiet prayer.

Themes found in this prayer service are searching for Christ, finding Christ in others, praying for others, and finding Christ in the Scriptures.

Note: This prayer service is a good one for kicking off a weekend retreat or for the start of a year with a youth group.

Supplies

Assorted religious artwork; index cards; a pen; three Bibles; a basket; a small table; slips of paper; a candle; matches; the song "You Have Been Baptized in Christ," by Carey Landry; sheets of paper

Preparation

Collect an assortment of religious artwork—for example, a painting of Christ, a crucifix, a statue of Mary, children's drawings, holy cards, and youth banners. Place the pieces of art all around the prayer space.

Write the word *Christ* on quarter pieces of index cards and hide them around the room—under plants, in books, behind chairs, and so forth. If you plan to hold this prayer service outside, make sure to hide the *Christ* cards within distinguishable boundaries.

Ask three teens to prepare to do the scriptural readings.

Immediately before the prayer service, while the young people are still milling around, make this announcement:

> Before we start prayer, look around the room, find Christ, and then you may come and sit down.

Some will find the cards with Christ's name on them; others may grab a crucifix or another symbol. Hopefully, some will find another person.

When everyone is seated, place slips of paper with the participants' names on them in a basket on a small table in the middle of the gathering. Place a candle on the table also. Then hand out songbooks and sheets listing the order of prayer.

Procedure

Call to prayer: Light the candle and say the following to the group:

> Sometimes we have to search for Christ in our lives. Often we overlook his presence in ourselves and in our neighbor.

Invite the group to sing "You Have Been Baptized in Christ," by Carey Landry (refrain only).

First reading: Matt. 3:16–17 (the baptism of Jesus)

Pause for quiet reflection: After the pause for quiet reflection, read the following prayer:

> Lord, God revealed your glory to all on the day of your baptism. Help us to see your glory in the gifts of each person gathered here.

Invite the group to sing "You Have Been Baptized in Christ" (refrain only).

Second reading: Mark 15:37–39 (Jesus' death on the cross)

Pause for quiet reflection: After the pause for quiet reflection, read the following prayer:

> Lord, you suffered and died on the cross so we might have the promise of salvation. Help us to see you in those who suffer and need our comfort.

Invite the group to sing "You Have Been Baptized in Christ" (refrain only).

Third reading: Luke 24:28–31 (the disciples on the road to Emmaus)

Pause for quiet reflection: After the pause for quiet reflection, read the following prayer:

> Lord, the disciples discovered your presence through the breaking of the bread. Help us to see you in each other as we break bread at meals and in the celebration of the Eucharist.

Invite the group to sing "You Have Been Baptized in Christ" (refrain only).

Exchange of prayer partners: Pass around the basket containing the slips with the participants' names and instruct everyone to take a name. Encourage everyone to pray especially for the person whose name they've chosen, asking God to enable the person to find Christ in herself or himself and others. Do not reveal the identities of the prayer partners.

Call to continued prayer: Explain that this service has no closing song or closing prayer because, it is hoped, the group will continue their prayer and discovery of Christ whenever they are together.

8
Prayer in Different Settings: New Places, New Inspirations

Overview

Think for a minute: Where is your favorite place to pray? In church, in the car, on a walk? Do you have a place you go regularly for prayer—a place like the beach, the mountains, a forest?

When I look back at my life, I realize that being near running water calls me to prayer like nothing else does. While I have been known to pray at fifty-five miles per hour on the interstate and in the midst of a room full of screaming teenagers, alongside a stream is the best place for me to tune in to the Lord.

When I was a youngster, the "crick" (that is what folks from Philadelphia called it) was more than just a place to skip stones in the summer and ice skate in the winter. I had a thinking tree there and would sit in it for hours with my feet dangling over the water, composing poetry and talking to God.

When I was a teenager and young adult, I used to take long walks along the creek at the camp where I worked, dreaming about the future and asking God to help me figure out what to do with my life.

Now that my parents have retired to Florida, the big attraction there is not the sights in Orlando; rather, it is the beach, for walking and praying in times of change.

Being selective in choosing settings can be an exciting way to vary prayer experiences with teens. If you haven't done so already, get your teens out of the pews and onto the floor. Use your imagination and theirs to seek new settings for prayer.

Different settings can

- show teens that prayer does not have to be confined to what we call "traditional holy places," like chapels and churches proper
- help teens discover their own "holy ground" for prayer
- intrigue and excite teens about a particular topic for prayer
- offer a comfortable place both to pray individually and to share prayer in groups
- help teens find new places and new times for working prayer into their busy lifestyle
- show young people that prayer, with a little imagination, can be a lot of fun

Take a look at the setting you normally use for prayer. I remember a youth group that used a big colorful room with throw pillows for its meetings, but then held prayer in a dark, formal church full of pews. And the youth group leaders wondered why the group was unresponsive.

Many teens love to decorate. They will be happy to help create a comfortable space for group prayer. Maybe they can convert a classroom or even a corner of a large room into a prayer space by decorating the walls and using throw pillows and comfortable chairs.

When asking teens to help prepare a prayer service, form a committee to work solely on the setting. Have them decorate your prayer space differently for each different prayer theme.

We have two chapels at our retreat center, but the "little" retreat chapel is the favorite. The walls are covered with small multicolored banners made by previous retreat groups. The pews are movable and shaped in a semicircle, but most often the teens just sit on the rug. No one is ever far away from the altar, and everyone can easily see and hear each other during shared prayer.

Look around your community, especially at the parks, for possible settings for prayer experiences. Why not take a field trip to a place just for a prayer experience? A different space may give new meaning to a scriptural passage and help teens connect the passage with modern-day experience. I remember a time when I shared in a prayer around a camp fire: We started our prayer with a walk through the dark woods to a clearing where only a small ember glowed in a fire circle. The scriptural passage was "'You are like light for the whole world . . .'" (Matt. 5:14–16). One by one we added wood to the growing fire while offering our prayers and promises of how we could help the light of Christ shine. Our prayer and fellowship transformed a few sparks into a mighty blaze. Being a light of Christ to the world took on a whole new meaning for all of us.

Guidelines

1. Check out a new site prior to prayer to make sure it is safe and usable.
2. Obtain permission when using any site, whether publicly or privately owned.
3. Consult the young people about what would make their prayer setting more comfortable.
4. When using the Scriptures for prayer, look for scriptural clues that will help you decorate the setting so that it might add to the understanding of the passages you use.
5. Use your imagination. Try to visualize the setting that would be most conducive to the prayer you are planning, and then find a way to create it.
6. Do not decorate a space to the point where it detracts and distracts from prayer.
7. Keep all five senses in mind when planning a prayer experience. What do you want the teens to see, hear, touch, smell, or taste?
8. Establish a regular prayer space for your group.
9. Encourage the teens to set aside a special space for their personal, private prayer.

Prayer Starters

1. Take the teens to a vineyard for a prayer service on Jesus as the true vine and us as the branches (John 15:5). See how wine is made and bring back a bottle to use as altar wine for a group Mass.
2. Hold a prayer service on "'I am the bread of life'" (John 6:35) in or near a bakery, where the sweet scent of bread can waft through the prayer space.
3. Celebrate Mass outside, with the trees for a cathedral and the soft grass for pews.
4. Bring pillows into the sanctuary of the church and sit on the floor. Gather around the pulpit for the liturgy of the word and around the altar for the liturgy of the Eucharist.
5. Start with a completely bare room and decorate it to go with the theme of the liturgy for the day.
6. For a liturgy, prepare and wear attire similar to what the Apostles might have worn. Re-enact the Last Supper.
7. Take a several-mile bike trip and hold different parts of a prayer service in different places along the way.
8. Take a ski lift to the top of a mountain for a prayer service on how God can help us climb even the highest mountain. Ski down for the grand finale.
9. Celebrate small-group liturgies in the homes of people in your group.
10. Attend morning Sabbath services at a synagogue. Arrange for the rabbi to answer questions afterward.
11. Arrange for the Roman Catholic members of your group to attend a Greek Orthodox or Byzantine liturgy, and arrange for Greek Orthodox or Byzantine members to attend a Roman Catholic liturgy. Share a dialog afterward.

12. If the members of your group or class belong to different parishes, rotate prayer services among the parishes so the teens can celebrate with other communities.

13. In the chapel of a hospital, hold a special prayer service for the sick. Arrange to visit and read to the patients in the children's ward afterward.

14. Go to a desert or a desertlike area and read the passage about Jesus going out to the desert to pray (Mark 1:35–39).

15. Serve a meal at a homeless shelter. After the meal, invite the people at the shelter to share a simple prayer service that has been prepared.

16. Offer a prayer on the court or field before a big game.

17. Visit a country fair and take time there to thank God for the many gifts of the earth.

18. During a long bus trip with your group, stop at a rest area and celebrate a short prayer service around the phrase "'Come to me, all of you who are tired . . . and I will give you rest'" (Matt. 11:28).

19. Hold a prayer service on the main concourse of a local mall. Focus on the snares and traps of materialism.

20. Hold a progressive meal at the homes of several teens. Share part of a progressive grace at each location.

21. Hold a night prayer service outside under the stars.

22. In conjunction with a tour of the newsroom of a local newspaper, hold a prayer service on Jesus, the Good News.

23. Work to make your parish church setting or school chapel more accessible to persons who are physically disabled, so they feel comfortable and welcome as worshiping members of the community.

24. Hold a Christmas Eve liturgy in an old barn filled with hay.

Prayer Service   "The House Built on Sand"

Featuring the Use of a Different Setting

In addition to prayer in a different setting, other prayer forms found in this prayer service are symbols, creative prayer, shared prayer, scriptural prayer, and quiet prayer.

Themes found in this prayer service are the future, facing struggles in life, reflecting on our life, faith journey, and building faith in God.

Supplies

Two sheets of paper, a pen or a typewriter, waterproof plastic covering for the sheets of paper, a sandy beach

Preparation

Write or type the two scriptural passages for the readings onto separate pieces of paper and cover them with waterproof plastic.

Choose a stretch of beach that has a large area of sand. An uncrowded area is preferable.

Note: If the beach is an ocean beach, plan to hold the first part of the prayer service during the part of the day when the tide is far out and the second part of the service after the tide has come in and washed away the sand castles the teens will have built earlier.

You may want to use the first part of this prayer at the beginning of a trip to the shore and use the second part right before you leave for home.

Procedure

First call to prayer: Ask the teens, working either alone or in groups, to start building sand castles. Make sure they work fairly close together and a decent distance from the water's edge. Allow them to work for ten minutes before continuing with the prayer service.

Shared prayer: Introduce the shared prayer as follows:

> Continue working on your castle, but think for a few moments about a prayer inspired by the creation in front of you. What are you building in your life right now? What goals are you seeking? What hurdles do you face?
>
> Perhaps your life project is not going quite as planned. Your obstacle may be a lack of building materials or a lack of ideas. What do you lack in your effort to build your life right now?
>
> As you think of a prayer, please offer it aloud, and we will join silently as a group in offering your prayer to God and praying for you. No one *has* to share a prayer, but I encourage you all to join in your own way.

First reading: John 8:3–8 (the woman accused of adultery and Jesus writing in the sand)

Reflection: Read the following reflection to the group:

> Have you ever wondered what Jesus was writing in the sand? Nowhere do we have an account of what he was writing or how long he wrote in the sand. Some say he was writing down the sins of the woman's accusers; others say he was writing down the good the woman had inside her that would later redeem her. Still others say he was writing a prayer asking God's forgiveness on our behalf. What do you think Jesus was writing? And if Jesus were to write in the sand about your life, what do you think he would write?

Writings in the sand: Invite the teens to reflect further on the first reading and spread out along the beach to write in the sand any thoughts or feelings triggered by the passage.

Second call to prayer: A second call to prayer can be made if the beach is an ocean beach and the tide has come in. If so, ask the teens to gather near the place where the castles once stood and where they can watch the waves coming in during prayer.

Reflection: Lead the following reflection for the group:

> Pick up some sand in your hand and study it for a moment. It is made up of tiny fragments that, with a little water and a lot of help, can be molded and shaped, if only for a while.
>
> In many ways, we are like the sand. Each of us is made up of so many different things and thoughts and ideas and aspects of personality. The waters of our baptism change and mold us too as they set us on a journey of faith.
>
> Sand, although fragile, is used to make glass and mirrors, objects we can look through to see our world and look into to see ourselves. Sand can also be used to make cement, a strong material on which buildings draw their foundation.

Second reading: Ask everyone to take a handful of sand and let it slowly run out between their fingers as someone reads Matt. 7:24–27 (the two house builders).

Reflection: Invite the group to reflect quietly on their own personal faith. Is it more like rock, or is it more like sand? Challenge them to think of ways they can strengthen their faith as the foundation of their life.

Closure: End the prayer service with a renewal of the baptismal promises and a dash into the waves for a quick swim.

9
Quiet Prayer:
Being Alone with God

Overview

Quiet prayer time at the retreat center is the only time I am sure I must be speaking in a foreign language. I carefully give directions to spread out so each person has plenty of space for this form of prayer. As soon as I finish giving directions, the teens all sit in clumps—right next to each other, sometimes even five people on a three-person couch. And then I, often with the aid of other adults, rearrange them so they are farther apart.

Young people like to move in crowds and make a lot of noise. That is just the way they are, and to some extent, this trait should be celebrated. But all of us, including teens, also need some time to be alone with our thoughts, some time to be alone with our prayer, and a chance to be quiet with God.

Quiet prayer can

- help settle teens down and enable them to focus on the present
- remove from a crowd some of the peer pressure that may put prayer down as not being cool
- allow some space in teens' busy, hectic world for Jesus to enter and touch their life

- help teens discover the comfort and serenity found in being silent with God
- offer a chance for teens to think through their everyday experiences and connect them with the words of the Gospel
- help set the stage for a personal prayer life that, hopefully, will become a lifetime habit

Teens often resist quiet prayer at first, but they are glad later to have had the quiet time. In this crazy, chaotic, loud world we live in, quiet time is not commonly sought after. We need to think of it both as a skill to be taught and a tradition to pass along.

I try to find small bits of quiet time every day—turning off the car radio to pray, or taking the quiet time right before going to bed at night. In recent years, I have tried to give myself a special gift on my birthday: I take a day off from all work, take the phone off the hook, and just relish the quiet for a while.

One of my most memorable experiences with quiet prayer happened during a wilderness survival training course with Colorado Outward Bound. My favorite part of the entire experience was the solo: We each had one entire day separate from the others in our group, to spend alone in the wilderness. The chance to rest and having the Rocky Mountains for a backdrop played an important role in my day, no doubt, but that experience of being alone and quiet with my God is something I wish I could recapture again and again.

I like to give teens something to help them focus during quiet prayer time, especially when it is a new experience for them. Reflection questions or a scriptural passage can serve this purpose. On longer retreats, I often hand out prayer journals, and although the teens are welcome to write in them at any time during the retreat, I find that they write in them mostly during quiet prayer time.

Space is required for quiet prayer, and young people each have a different way of creating their own space. Some curl up on big windowsills or sprawl on the floor. Outside, they will sit under a tree or perch atop a picnic table. I once was startled by a teen curled up in a closet. He wasn't asleep, and I couldn't disagree that he had indeed found a spot that was quiet—were it not for a certain retreat director who likes to close closet doors that are ajar.

Guidelines

1. Encourage the teens to respect and honor quiet time for themselves and others.
2. Make quiet prayer a regular part of your group's meetings, classes, or retreats so the teens grow accustomed to it.
3. As an adult, respect the teens' use of quiet time. Nothing is more distracting to them than a knot of adult leaders chatting while the teens are supposed to be quiet.
4. Adjust the length of time for quiet prayer to match the quiet time capacity of the group you are working with. Increase the amount of time as the teens grow more comfortable with it.
5. Vary the length of time for quiet prayer to suit the occasion. Five minutes may be fine for reflecting on a retreat witness talk, while a

longer period of quiet time is needed for preparing for the sacrament of reconciliation.

6. Give the teens, especially those new to quiet prayer, a reading or a writing task to help them focus during their quiet time.

7. Make sure the teens have plenty of room to spread out and find their own space. If your room is too small, use two rooms. If teens are packed too close together, it is almost impossible for them to stay quiet for very long.

Prayer Starters

1. Compile booklets of poems, prayers, stories, and reflections for use during quiet prayer time.

2. If weather permits, ask the teens to find a place outside to sit for quiet prayer. Invite them to close their eyes or put on a blindfold and listen to the sounds and experience the touch and smell of the God's creation around them.

3. Schedule an entire afternoon or a several-day retreat for older teens and young adults to spend in quiet prayer.

4. Give each of the teens paper and a pencil to write a letter to God during quiet prayer time, inviting God into their life. Have them put the letters in self-addressed envelopes, and then send the letters back to the teens after a few months.

5. Hold a three-hour silent retreat with time scheduled afterward to discuss how difficult it is, in today's society, to make time for quiet prayer and to become comfortable with being quiet.

6. Give each teen a Bible with passages already marked to read during quiet prayer time. The passages could relate to the theme of your meeting or lead into your next discussion.

7. Show a "message" film designed to really make the teens think. Hand out questions for them to work on during quiet prayer time.

8. Give each of the teens a lump of clay. Ask them to create, in silence, something that signifies their relationship with God.

9. Ask the teens to volunteer to watch children in the church crying room so parents can experience a few moments of quiet and peacefulness during Sunday liturgy.

10. Allow a few moments of quiet time after each witness talk on a retreat, so the teens can reflect and write in a prayer journal.

11. Show a clip of a film without the sound. Ask the teens to prayerfully reflect on what they have seen and what they might have heard if the sound had been on.

12. Allow the teens time to walk around outside, in silence, in an area with a varied terrain. Then gather together for shared prayer, each person starting with the phrase "The gift I found in the quiet was . . ."

13. Tell the teens to write down the amount of quiet they find in a typical day, when and where it occurs, and how they use it. Challenge them to increase that amount of time and make better use of it.

14. Ask relatives, friends, and parishioners to write palancas (letters of support) for your young people. Surprise the young people by handing out the palancas for reading during quiet prayer time.

15. For night prayer on an outdoor retreat or camping trip, tell the teens to lie on their back and explore the stars with their eyes and reflect silently on God's wonderful gift of creation.

16. Ask the teens to consider how they make use of quiet time at Mass, especially the time after Communion.

17. On a week- or weekend-long retreat, give each of the retreatants a copy of a stations of the cross booklet. Ask them to make a silent pilgrimage through the stations, to be completed by the end of the retreat. This is ideal for Lent, especially if your site has outdoor stations.

18. Read the popular poem "Footprints" and ask the teens to reflect quietly on a time in their life when Jesus carried them or a situation in their life right now where they need to be able to hold on to Jesus.

19. Be a ghost writer for God and write a personalized letter to each teen. A word processor will make this task easier. Give the teens some quiet time to read the letters and write a response.

20. Schedule quiet time for the teens to write an examination of conscience based on their experiences in school, at work, and at home. Collect the examinations of conscience together in a booklet for other teens to use while preparing to receive the sacrament of reconciliation.

21. Make a collection of the favorite prayers of saints, or even the favorite prayers of celebrities, and put them in a booklet for the teens to read during their personal quiet time at home.

22. For a quiet prayer exercise, give the teens a selection of Dear Abby clippings from the paper. Ask them to pick one and write a prayer about the problem or issue found there.

23. Give each of the teens a few large strips of construction paper and ask them to write a prayer of petition on each strip during quiet time. Later, link everyone's strips together in a large paper chain as a sign of the power of prayer in the community.

24. Share a nonverbal sign of peace, each person greeting another with a sign of peace or affection without saying a word.

Prayer Service "What Do You Need for the Journey?"

Featuring the Use of Quiet Prayer

In addition to quiet prayer, other prayer forms found in this prayer service are symbols, scriptural prayer, and shared prayer.

Themes found in this prayer service are journeying with God, "the Scriptures speak to us," following the light of Christ, "bread can nourish the soul," and the invitation of baptism.

Note: This prayer service is designed for seniors graduating from high school. It can be adapted for other occasions that mark a departure time.

Supplies

A small table, a nice tablecloth, a Christ candle, matches, a box of taper candles, small bread rolls, a basket, a crystal bowl, water, a towel, a Bible, slips of paper, a pen or a typewriter, a piece of paper, Bibles, pencils

Preparation

Divide the prayer space into four areas. Place a small table in the center of the entire space. Cover the table with a nice cloth. Light a Christ candle on the table and place a box of taper candles nearby. Arrange small bread rolls in a basket. Fill a crystal bowl with water and place a towel nearby. Open a Bible and surround it with slips of paper with the following passages written out on them:
- John 8:12 (Jesus, the light of the world)
- Luke 8:16–18 (a lamp under a bowl)
- Matt. 25:1–13 (the parable of the ten girls)
- Matt. 6:22–23 (the light of the body)
- John 6:33–35 ("'I am the bread of life.'")
- Luke 22:19 ("'This is my body.'")
- John 6:1–13 (the loaves and fish)
- Luke 13:20–21 (the parable of the yeast)
- Matt. 14:22–33 (Jesus walking on the water)
- Luke 8:22–25 (Jesus calming a storm)
- John 13:4–14 (Jesus washing the disciples' feet)
- Mark 1:9–11 (the baptism of Jesus)

Note: Consider asking any teens who help plan prayer to suggest other symbols and scriptural passages for the prayer table.

Prepare a reflection sheet by writing or typing the following words on a piece of paper:

Water, Light, Word, and Bread—
Powerful Symbols for the Journey

Read John 21:1–14. Reflect on and then answer the following questions:
1. How does water play an important role in this story?
   How does the water of baptism influence your faith journey?
2. How does fire play an important role in this story?
   How does the light of Christ impact your faith story?
3. How do the words of Jesus affect the disciples in this story?
   Are you open to God's word in your life?
4. How does Jesus feed the disciples in this story?
   How does Jesus feed you in body and soul?
5. What message does Jesus have for you in this story, that you can take with you and use on your journey?

Make enough photocopies of the reflection sheet for everyone who will participate. Ask the teens to enter the prayer space quietly and gather in a circle around the small table.

Procedure

Call to prayer: Say something like the following to the group:

> Each of us is about to embark on a journey. We leave behind the security and routine of the last four years and take separate paths to jobs or college, which take us to different places and new experiences.
>
> We do not go alone. We go with God. Let us reflect now on what we need to take with us on our journey. Think about what it is you need, and when you are ready, come forward and share a symbol of that need.
>
> If you need the word of God, come forth and take one of the scriptural passages written on these slips of paper. If you need the light of Christ to show you the way, take a taper candle and light it from the Christ candle.
>
> If you need bread to fill a physical or spiritual hunger, come forth and break a piece of bread and eat it. If you need water to refresh or cleanse you, come forth and wash your hands in the water or splash some on your face.

Ask the teens to come forward in any order, one at a time, until all have had a chance to take something for their journey. Ask them to remain quiet throughout the experience.

Individual reflection: Give each of the teens a Bible, a copy of the reflection sheet, and a pencil. Ask them to spread out throughout the room, read the scriptural passage referred to on the sheet, and write their answers to the reflection questions on the sheet.

Gifts for the journey: Gather the teens together in a circle and ask them to reflect on a gift they would like to share with another for the journey ahead.

Start the sharing by motioning for one teen to come forward to the prayer table. Tell him or her to choose one of the four gifts to share with any other person who is present. He or she may light and share a candle, share a scriptural passage, break bread with the other person, or wash the person's hands as a sign of service.

After the first gift-giver returns to his or her seat, the person who received a gift now gives one away. Continue until everyone has been gifted for the journey.

Closure: Invite the group to offer a nonverbal sign of peace to each other. Afterward, they may leave the room or chapel quietly.

10
Storytelling: Praying Stories of Faith

Overview

Each of our lives is a story written daily, word by word, page by page, as we move along the journey of life. It is a story of faith that, when shared with others, can be a powerful prayer—a powerful way to lift hearts and minds to God. Within each of us are found stories of conversion and the people, events, and everyday miracles that have brought us closer to Christ.

The sharing of faith stories, especially among teens, is one of the most powerful forms of evangelization that can be found. I have been moved and humbled time and time again by listening to young people's stories of faith during witness talks on retreats. Sometimes they have told their faith stories at great personal risk—like the one who told of trying to commit suicide and fighting her way back from depression through a growing reliance on God.

I have heard teens talk about how they used drugs or sex or fell into anorexia while trying to fill an empty space inside—then to realize that only God can make us truly feel whole and love us the way we are. I never really understood the Beatitude "Happy are those who mourn" until I heard a teen talk about losing his brother in a stabbing and how his faith helps him keep going and keeps his brother's memory alive.

Storytelling can

- trigger emotion by touching a person in her or his own experience of joy, sorrow, anticipation, fear
- surprise us and challenge us to look at a problem or issue in a new way
- invite us to step outside our own worldview and walk in the shoes of another for a while
- provide a connection between the human and the divine
- allow us a chance to find the real persons below the surface of ordinary conversation
- enable us to retell our own story through the characters found in the stories of others

Sharing your own faith story is not easy, but teens need and want to hear the faith stories of the adults who minister to them.

Speaking about my own faith story is something that still remains difficult for me even after years of youth ministry work. Once, when invited to speak at a local high school, I ached to find a way to reach the teens on their own level. I was only ten years older than many of them at the time, but to them the chasm seemed enormous.

In my hour-long presentation, I told them a story about a high school student I had known—one who struggled with self-esteem, couldn't see her gifts, often suffered from depression. I talked about how she felt lost in her large high school, yearned to be part of the popular crowd, and just could not talk to her parents.

I continued to weave the story into the group discussion, music, and other activities throughout the workshop, telling the teens how this student finally, although slowly, realized that the missing piece in her life was God.

At the end of the workshop, I told them that the student was so proud to finish high school that she still wears her high school ring today. Then I held up my hand for them to see. And to my surprise . . . they cheered. I had built a bridge.

Our prayer can only become richer by learning more about our own story, sharing in the stories of others, and celebrating the Jesus story.

Guidelines

1. Be genuine when telling your own story; speak from the heart.
2. Use stories that are similar to your own or, better yet, stories that fit it into the life experience of the teens you are working with.
3. Scan *Reader's Digest* or *Catholic Digest* for anecdotes to add pizzazz to talks or introductions.
4. Keep a notebook handy just for collecting stories. Jot down good ones right after you hear them—in a homily, on television, or in a conversation.
5. *Tell* a story; try not to read it. Go over it a few times and even practice telling it. Become so familiar with it that you identify with the experiences the story relates.

6. Try different ways of telling stories. Use mime, drama, props, music, puppetry, and different settings.

7. Look for the humor in the stories' situations and bring out the funny parts whenever you can.

8. Use plenty of description to make the characters and scenes pop into the listeners' imagination. Description gives texture to a story.

Prayer Starters

1. Look for newspaper articles about people who have triumphed over adversity, and offer a prayer of thanksgiving for the real heroes of today.

2. If a story involves several characters, ask several different teens to take parts.

3. During a prayer service for engaged couples, invite a married couple to share the highs and lows of their life together.

4. Ask the teens to find a copy of their favorite childhood story. It could be one by Dr. Seuss or one their parents made up. Ask them to search for any faith messages they may find there.

5. Challenge the teens to tell a story mainly using excerpts from popular songs.

6. Help the teens get in touch with their own life story by writing their own obituary. What do they want it to say at the end of their long life?

7. Look for stories from other cultures and traditions. We can enrich our own spirituality by learning how others experience God.

8. Start a collection of life stories of saints, those who lived in the past or those who are still with us. For example, during a prayer service on vocations, share some anecdotes from Mother Teresa's life.

9. At the start of a retreat weekend, ask the participants to write down a short story about the struggles in their life. Leave all these stories in a basket before the Blessed Sacrament as a prayer for help and a chance to leave behind the burdens while seeking renewal.

10. During quiet time, use the story-poem "One Solitary Life" as a reflection on the story of Jesus and how his story has changed the life stories of others throughout history.

11. Tell the first half of a story to set the tone for a prayer service. Then conclude the prayer service with the rest of the story.

12. After telling a story, give the young people something concrete to reflect upon to help them remember the message you hope to share. For example, give each young person a rock after telling the story of Jesus calling Peter the rock on which the church will be built (Matt. 16:13–20).

13. Have the teens collect stories of faith from people of different ages. They can keep the stories in a prayer journal to reflect upon or share.

14. Choose one of the Gospel stories and tell it from the point of view of a lesser character. For example, tell the story of the ten lepers (Luke 17:11–19) from the viewpoint of one of the nine who didn't come back to say thank you to Jesus. Or tell the parable of the prodigal son (Luke 15:11–32) from the viewpoint of the older brother.

15. Create a prayer service around the theme "Never judge a book by its cover," with the point being that we need to find the "story in each person" before we can really get to know him or her.

Using Stories with Prayer Themes

The following are several stories and the prayer themes that I pulled from them. They are presented for your use, and also as examples of stories that can be used for prayer.

The Story: "The Dove and the Wise Old Man"

> Once there lived a very wise old man.
> People came from all around
> to seek advice
> and learn from his wisdom.
> There was another man who lived in the town,
> who was very jealous of the wise man
> and planned to trick him.
> He said: "I will go to the wise man
> with a dove concealed in my hands.
> I will ask the wise man if the dove
> is dead or alive.
> If he says the dove is alive,
> I will squeeze my hands together and kill it
> so the wise man will be wrong.
> If he says the dove is dead,
> I will open my hands and let it fly free
> so the wise man will be wrong."
> So he journeyed to the place where the wise man lived,
> held the dove between his hands, and asked,
> "Good teacher, tell me, is the dove dead or alive?"
> The wise man said,
> "It is what you make of it."
>
> (Author unknown)

The story's prayer themes

- Don't wait for others to make decisions for you.
- Protect the wonderful gifts God has given you.
- Be on guard against those who try to trip you up.
- What are you going to make out of your gift of life?

The Story: "The Starfish"

> As the old man walked the beach at dawn he noticed a youth ahead of him picking up starfish and flinging them into the sea. Finally, catching up with the youth, he asked him why he was doing this. The answer was that the stranded starfish would die if left in the morning sun. "But the beach goes on for miles and there are millions of starfish," countered the old man. "How can your effort make any difference?"
>
> The young man looked at the starfish in his hand and then threw it to the safety of the waves. "It makes a difference to this one," he said. (Anonymous, from *The Sower's Seeds*, by Brian Cavanaugh, p. 26)

The story's prayer themes
- Each person can make a difference.
- We must protect and preserve God's gifts found in the environment.
- Those who are older are not always wiser. Wisdom often comes from the young.
- Who are the people in our life who throw us back to safety when we feel stranded on the beach?

The Story: "Bundles of Worries, Bundles of Blessings"

A woman who worried day in, day out, made her family miserable with all her fears. One day she went to a wise friend. "I have more worries than anyone else in the world," she wailed. "Could you help me deal with them?"

"Only God can help you deal with your worries," said the wise friend. "Take your troubles to [God] and don't despair."

The woman followed her friend's advice and asked God for help. One night, she dreamed she was in a large gray cave filled with thousands of gray bundles. Some were big, some were small, and none were of the same size.

As she looked at the gray bundles, an old man came toward her and said, "These are worry bundles. All the people in the world carry one of those on their left shoulder. If you feel that your bundle is too heavy for you, put it down and choose one that suits you better."

The woman looked and saw that she was indeed carrying a gray bundle on her left shoulder. She put it down and began to search for a lighter one. She tried out hundreds of bundles until finally she found one that seemed just right.

"May I take this one?" she asked. "It feels much more comfortable than all the others."

"You may take whichever you want," the man answered kindly. "But open the bundle before you leave."

When the woman opened the bundle, she saw all of her worries inside. Well, she had picked her own worry bundle. She sighed deeply and said, "At least my own worry bundle fits me better than the other ones."

"That seems to be true for everyone," replied the man with a little smile. "But do not despair. There is a bundle on your other shoulder that should lighten your worries."

The woman looked and saw another bundle on her right shoulder. But it was not gray. It was woven from gold and silver threads, and it sparkled like a diamond in the sun. Just looking at it made her feel better.

"I wonder what is in it," she said excitedly.

"Why don't you open it?" the old man suggested.

She did and found that the bundle was filled to the top with all her blessings. As she looked at them, one after the other, her heart overflowed with thankfulness and gratitude. Full of joy, she turned toward the man to thank him for making her aware of the gold-and-silver bundle.

But the old man was gone, and so were the huge gray cave and all the worry bundles. The woman was in her own bed, and the beautiful morning sun was shining into her face. (*A Piece of the Wind: And Other Stories to Tell,* by Ruthilde Kronberg and Patricia C. McKissack, pp. 21–22)

The story's prayer themes
- God doesn't give us any burden that we cannot handle.
- Sometimes it is easier to see our burdens instead of our blessings.
- It is important to take time, stop, and count our blessings.
- We need to help others carry their burdens.
- What are some of the ways we can be blessings for others?

The Story: "Two Brothers"

Two brothers shared a farm. The younger brother was married and had seven children. The older brother was single. They worked hard on land that was good. So for many years the harvests were abundant, and each year the brothers split the wealth of the land evenly. Thanking God for their prosperity, they gathered the grain into separate barns.

After one harvesttime, the older, single brother thought to himself: "It is not right that we should divide the grain evenly. My brother has many mouths to feed, and he needs more. I have only myself to look after. I can certainly get by with less." So each night the single brother would take grain from his barn and secretly transfer it to the married brother's barn.

That same night, the married brother thought to himself: "It is not right that we should divide the grain evenly. I have many children who will look after me in my old age. My brother has only himself. Surely he will need to save more for the future." So each night the married brother would take grain from his barn and secretly transfer it to his older brother's barn.

So, as it happened, each night the brothers gave away their grain; yet each morning they found their supply mysteriously replenished. Neither brother told the other about this miraculous happening.

Then one night after a month or so, the brothers met each other halfway between the barns. They realized at once what was happening. They embraced one another with laughter and tears. And on that spot they built a temple in which to worship God. (Adapted from a story retold in *An Experience Named Spirit,* by John Shea)

The story's prayer themes
- Those who are willing to give shall also receive.
- It is good to be humble when giving; give without expecting anything in return.
- God creates miracles in our very midst.
- Justice is defined differently by different people.
- Those with plenty have a responsibility to give to those who are in need.

The Story: "'And Then What?'"

There once was an old teacher, working in her garden. On this day, she was busying weeding so her vegetables would be able to grow strong and high and reach for the sun. One of her students rushed up, breathless, and announced: "I have discovered what I want to do with my life. I want to go to law school."

The old woman looked up and said, "And then what?"

"Well, then I want to graduate at the very top of my class—with honors," the student said.

The old teacher said, "And then what?"

"I want to be the best lawyer anywhere around, get the best cases, win the most trials, be famous far and wide," said the student.

The old gardener said, "And then what?"

"I want to make lots of money, buy a fast car and my own house," said the young woman.

The old teacher said, "And then what?"

"I want to meet a great guy, get married, and have some children . . . but not too many, so I'll be able to keep working."

The old woman said, "And then what?"

"I want to go into politics, get into the state legislature, maybe even run for governor one day."

The old gardener said, "And then what?"

"I want to buy a house in Florida and retire."

The old teacher said, "And then what?"

"Well, I guess I'll die. Everyone does."

"And then what?"

"Well, I guess I'll face judgment."

"And then what?"

And the young woman went home and changed her plans.

And the old teacher went back to working in her garden. She pulled out the weeds one by one so the plants would be able to grow strong and high and reach for the sun. (Adapted from a retreat homily given by Fr. Phil Rodgers)

The story's prayer themes

- Society has a great influence on our perception of what it means to be successful.
- What does it really mean to be successful?
- The simple things in life are often the most valuable.
- Which is more important—people or things?
- It is never too late to change your plans.

Prayer Service "'View from the Balcony'"

Featuring the Use of Storytelling

In addition to storytelling, other prayer forms found in this prayer service are music, quiet prayer, shared prayer, and scriptural prayer.

Themes found in this prayer service are "Love your neighbor," "Respect all life, especially the elderly," putting faith into action, the call to service, and God's intimate concern for all of us.

Supplies

Slips of paper; a pen; a basket; a Bible; a recording of "Another Day in Paradise," by Phil Collins; a tape player or CD player

Preparation

Ask an older teen to prepare a fifteen-minute witness talk on her or his first experience of visiting elderly persons in a nursing home. The points for the teen to bring out in the story are as follows:
• the anxiety and fears about going to a nursing home and the initial uncomfortableness about being around those who are very old
• how rewarding the experience of visiting elderly persons can be
• that many people in the nursing home are glad for the company or a chance to share their story
• what one particular resident did or said that has touched the teen's life in a special way
• how the entire experience of the nursing home has affected the teen's faith

Obtain the names of residents of a nursing home in your neighborhood. Write the name of each resident on a slip of paper and place all the slips of paper in a basket. If it is possible to have your group visit the nursing home, plan to do so in the near future.

Ask a teen to prepare to read the story "View from the Balcony," found in the procedure section of this prayer service.

Ask a teen to prepare to read the scriptural passage that will close the prayer service.

Procedure

Call to prayer: Play "Another Day in Paradise," by Phil Collins.

The story: "View from the Balcony"

An 84-year-old woman sat for two months on her balcony this winter before a neighbor discovered she was dead, it was reported yesterday.

The woman may have died while watching fireworks from her apartment on New Year's Eve, police in the Stockholm suburb of Traneberg said.

The woman was found Monday sitting on a chair on her balcony, dressed in a coat and hat. Her forehead was leaning against the railing.

Margaretha Marsellas, a neighbor, realized something was wrong when she saw the woman on the balcony around the clock despite freezing temperatures.

"I accused myself for not having seen her earlier. . . . I hope this dreadful story makes us better at keeping in touch with our old neighbors," Marsellas was quoted as telling an Aftonbladet newspaper. ["Woman Found Dead After 2 Months on Balcony," Stockholm, Sweden (AP), 16 March 1992]

Note: An alternative to using this story is to find one closer to the teens' experience. Try to find a similar one in your local newspaper.

Pause for silent reflection: This reflection can be nondirected, or it can be directed toward reflecting on a time when the individuals at the service "walked by" instead of stopping to help someone in need. A prayer for the courage to stop and make a difference can also be silently prayed.

Prayers of petition: Invite prayers of petition for elderly relatives and ask all to respond to the prayers with "Lord, never let us forget your love."

Witness talk: Invite the older teen to tell the group the story about her or his first visit to a nursing home.

Prayer response: Pass around the basket containing the slips with the names of nursing home residents on them. Ask the young people to pick a name and to offer a silent prayer for the person whose name they picked. If the young people are to visit the nursing home, remind them to pray for that person in a special way the week before the visit.

Closure: Signal for the previously chosen teen to read Isa. 49:13–16.

11
Audiovisuals: High-Tech Prayer

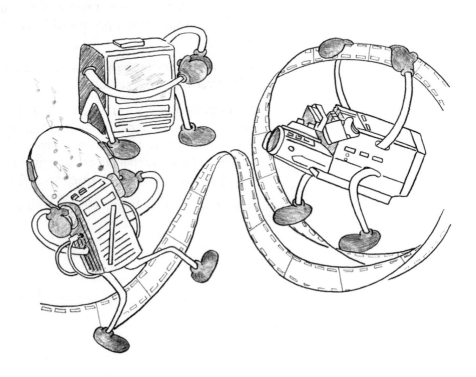

Overview

I get a kick out of telling teens that I do not own a television. Their astonishment—that someone could live in the 1990s and survive without a TV—is a good indicator of the influence of television and how much audiovisuals, generally, have become part of the fabric of our culture.

Likewise, I remember the shocked looks of the adults when a priest rolled out a big-screen TV and used a music video as part of his homily during a youth Mass. The video highlighted and reinforced the Gospel message for that day. The teens talked about that homily for weeks. It really made an impact.

Audiovisuals can

- give sight and sound to abstract concepts
- create a setting or mood to make teens more open to prayer
- meet young people in some of their favorite media and challenge them to pray in a different way

- meet teens where they are at and connect the need for prayer with their everyday life
- help teens deal with real-life issues through the eyes of another

Prayer using audiovisuals often takes more preparation than other forms of prayer. Failure to prepare usually leads to situations that are humorous only long after they have occurred.

When leading one retreat at a parish some distance from the retreat center where I work, I had asked that a projector be provided for the film that was the centerpiece of the program. During the retreat, I found that the projector had an unusual system for threading the film, but I was sure I had it figured out. When I turned on the projector, we had a picture . . . but no sound. While the teens sat and fidgeted, I searched for someone in the parish building who knew how to operate the device. Even after that we were able to get only a minimum amount of sound. We must have looked pretty funny—all crowded together near the projector with ears cocked toward it.

Guidelines

1. Make sure you know how to operate the piece of audiovisual equipment you are going to use. Always test the equipment before you use it.

    If planning to use a *VCR,* check to make sure it is connected to the cable and to the television. Find out which television channel the VCR plays on.

    If planning to use a *film projector,* learn how to thread the machine properly to avoid jumping pictures or damage to the film. Check the volume controls to learn where they should be set to get the volume you want.

    If planning to use a *slide projector,* make sure slides drop properly from the carousel and come back up. If you are going to play music with the slides, make sure the slides and the music are coordinated.

    In all of these situations, make sure the operator's manual will be handy or that someone who is familiar with the equipment will be nearby.

2. Order a film or video early enough for it to arrive for previewing.

3. Check to see if your diocese has a film and video library. If it does, take a day to preview some of the offerings.

4. Make sure you have any needed auxiliary equipment: adapter plugs, spare light bulbs, extension cords, take-up reels, and batteries.

5. If you ask teens to bring music for a prayer service, make sure you have the right equipment to play it: a CD player, a tape player, a turntable, or whatever.

6. Make sure all the teens can see the screen when using a video or film. If a big-screen TV is available, use it when showing a video to a group of more than twenty people.

7. Check the volume capacity of the equipment you are using to make sure the sound will be audible for the size of the room and the size of the audience. Consider additional speakers for a larger group.

8. Always view a film before using it with the teens. Do not rely solely on a written description. I have often viewed a film that sounded

good, but then realized it was not really appropriate for the age-group or the theme of the prayer service I was preparing.

Do not be afraid to use a film or video that the teens have seen before—they often watch a favorite film time and again. Try using the film or video in different ways. I have found new meaning in films I have seen several times. One video I have seen over and over is part of one of my most popular retreat programs. It still moves me to tears the same way it did the first time I saw it. Good films are like good stories: they often yield their message in the retelling.

Prayer Starters

1. Use a clip of a movie the teens have seen and discussed before, as a bridge to a prayer service on a related theme.
2. Show a film to set the tone or theme for prayer. If the film has a high emotional content, move right into prayer as the movie ends. There is a safeness in the dark that makes teens feel comfortable; you may even want to remain in the dark for the prayer or keep the lights dim for shared prayer.
3. On a retreat, consider using a video in place of night prayer, especially one with a surprise ending that challenges the teens to think. It is a nice way to end the day.
4. Put a slide in a projector and cover an entire wall of the prayer space with one scene to create a setting or special mood for prayer, or change the slide two or three times during different parts of a prayer service.
5. Give the teens themselves time to prepare a videotape, acting out a scriptural passage. Show the video later as part of a prayer experience.
6. Instead of using just the music of a contemporary song, use the music video also, if the visual message matches the theme of the prayer service you are planning.
7. Show half of a video to open a prayer service and then end the prayer service with the other half.
8. Take photos of your group or class throughout the school year. For a year-end prayer service, create a slide show to the words of one of the teens' favorite songs.
9. Ask the teens to write prayers inspired by music videos. Start classes or group meetings with one of the prayers paired with the video that inspired it.
10. Ask the teens to think about a movie they have seen recently and the message of faith they discovered there.
11. Obtain some slides from the Holy Land and scatter the viewing of them throughout a prayer service on walking in the steps of Jesus.
12. Ask the teens' parents to give you slides from their family gatherings. Surprise the teens by showing the slides during a prayer service on families. If families have only photos available, slides can be made from the photos.
13. Fill up a sixty-minute audiocassette with favorite spiritual songs, readings, and sayings—all performed by members of your group. Use the cassette in prayer services, for sharing with shut-ins, or for sending to relatives and friends who have moved away.

14. Have the group record their reflections on Christian messages found in contemporary music. Add some of your group's favorite prayer ideas. Send the tape to a class or group in another state and ask them for a similar tape in return.

Using Clips from Popular Movies and Television Programs

Movies

Batman: The scene—Bruce Wayne struggles to reveal his identity to the woman he loves. He opens his mouth but can't quite find the courage to get the words out.

You may want to use this clip as part of a prayer service on "learning to reveal the true you."

Father of the Bride: The scene—the daughter tries to tell her father that she is engaged to be married. All he sees sitting in her chair is a little girl in pigtails.

This works well in a prayer experience on parent-teen relationships.

Dead Poets Society: The scene—in the courtyard, the teacher shows his students how to march to the beat of their own drummer.

The clip works well in a prayer service on peer pressure or standing up for what one believes in. The whole movie is a great portrayal about adolescence and coming of age.

Oh, God! The scene—the lead character meets God face-to-face for the first time.

The clip can lead into a guided meditation in which the young people imagine what they would do or say if God were revealed to them one day in the same way.

Beauty and the Beast (Walt Disney version): The scene—the Beast is injured, and Beauty rescues him and tends to his wounds.

This clip works well for the topic of self-image and self-esteem or taking the risk to really get to know a person.

Television Programs

"Highway to Heaven" and "I'll Fly Away": Look for scenes with messages rooted in the Scriptures or with a definite moral.

These clips work for centering prayer

Jesus of Nazareth: Instead of reading parables, use corresponding scenes from this TV miniseries.

These clips can be used for centering prayer.

Using Films with Religious Themes

Here is ordering information for the films in this section: The films *Pardon, Peace; Jingo;* and *Portraits* are distributed by Franciscan Communications, 1229 South Santee Street, Los Angeles, CA 90015. Phone 800-989-3600 or 213-746-2916. The film *The Man Who Mugged God* is distributed by Paulist Productions, P.O. Box 1057, Pacific Palisades, CA 90272. Phone 310-454-0688. Check your local audiovisual office for the availability of *The Giving Tree.*

Pardon, Peace (Franciscan Communications, 11 minutes): Pardon, Peace is about a runaway who has spurned his family and is afraid to go home. While hitchhiking, he meets a man who was never able to make peace with his parents. This encounter encourages the boy to go home, where he is amazed to be greeted with open arms.

- Use the first part of the film at the start of a reconciliation service. Use the homecoming after private confessions are over, to conclude the service.
- Show the film and ask the teens to write prayer-letters asking God for forgiveness.
- Show the film during a parent-teen retreat and lead into shared prayer, with the parents praying for the teens and the teens praying for the parents.

The Giving Tree (A Bosustow Production, 10 minutes): *The Giving Tree,* a timeless story, features a selfless tree that gives all it has to serve a demanding boy who grows into adulthood asking for more and more. The tree gives all of itself, until it is a mere stump, in order to make the boy happy.

- After showing the film, ask the teens to make a written pledge of service to the community. Have them hang their pledge on a small tree during the preparation of the gifts at liturgy.
- Encourage small groups of teens to write short prayers of thanks for all the marvelous gifts God has given us. Combine the prayers into a litany of thanksgiving to be read during prayer. Make a copy of the litany for each teen to take and use at home.
- Prepare an examination of conscience that helps the teens reflect on their own selfishness and the need to learn how to put others before themselves.

Jingo (Franciscan Communications, 12 minutes): *Jingo* is about a Vietnamese youth who juggles for a living. He is befriended by an old woman holding a twenty-dollar bill. After his performance she asks, "Have you earned it?" He is challenged to become the best juggler he can be and, in the process, discovers a unique friendship.

- Show this film during an agape prayer service and include a reflection on the different kinds of hunger—the hunger that we can satisfy with regular bread and the hunger that can be filled only by God.
- During a reflection on friendship, ask the teens to comment on Jingo's statement, "People who are amazed at you are not necessarily your friends."
- The woman in the film tells Jingo, "It is not the scarves you juggle that are beautiful; it is the way you handle them that is beautiful." Consider a reflection on how we sometimes need others to reflect the beauty found inside ourselves.

The Man Who Mugged God (Paulist Productions, 26 minutes): A common street thief gets more than he bargained for when he mugs an old blind man. The blind man offers the thief his coat, his money, and sanctuary from the police in his home. The blind man knows all about the mugger and retells his life story for him. The blind man finally reveals his own identity—God.

- Show the film right up through the part where the thief threatens God with a knife at his throat. Then stop the film and ask the teens to write their own ending. Talk about the teens' endings in small groups before playing the rest of the film.

- During quiet time, ask the teens to reflect on how they would react if one day they encountered God. Zero in on some of God's lines in the film: "If you run away from me, you are running away from yourself." "It does embarrass people to admit they believe in me." "Stop putting down what I raised up; I love you, so how can you be nothing?"
- Use the film as part of the preparation for a reconciliation service. Build your service around God's line from the film, "If I forgive you, you will have to forgive yourself."

Portraits (Franciscan Communications, 19 minutes): Amelia struggles with a class project requiring her to draw a self-portrait. She discards pictures of herself as a teen princess, a popularity star, and a best friend when embarrassments call into question her view of herself. She finally settles on a portrait of herself as she really is.

- Have the teens create paper masks with pictures and words on the outside to show how they want people to see them, to show the image they project.
- Pass a small hand mirror around the prayer circle, with each teen offering a prayer asking God to learn how to accept ourselves just as we were created.
- Ask the teens to reflect on the ways they cover up the real person inside themselves by the use of makeup, clothes, choice of friends, smoking, or alcohol.

Prayer Service "The Three Tests of Faith"

Featuring the Use of Audiovisuals

In addition to audiovisuals, other prayer forms found in this prayer service are music, symbols, scriptural prayer, quiet prayer, a traditional prayer, drama, prayer in different settings, and storytelling.

Themes found in this prayer service are humility, following Jesus, trusting in God, the risk of faith, learning from the Scriptures, seeking God's help, and "nothing is impossible with God."

Note: The basic outline of this prayer service can also be used as a format for a retreat day by adding activities, discussion, and witness talks to each of the three main parts.

Supplies

The video *Indiana Jones and the Last Crusade;* a television; a VCR; three Bibles; the *Indiana Jones and the Last Crusade* soundtrack (optional); paper; a pen or a typewriter; a recording of "Send Me an Angel," by Scorpions; a tape player or CD player

Preparation

Find the spot in *Indiana Jones and the Last Crusade,* about twenty minutes from the end of the movie, where Indiana Jones faces the three tests of faith. Cue up the tape to right before Indy's adversary says: "Okay, Dr. Jones. Now it is time to see what you really believe."

Run the tape through this section beforehand and note where to stop the tape in between the tests of faith. Make sure you are using a VCR with a pause button.

Ask three teens to prepare to do the scriptural readings for the prayer service.

Prepare prayer sheets with the prayer responses that will be used printed on them.

If the soundtrack from the movie is available on a CD or audiocassette, you may want to play it as the teens gather for prayer.

Procedure

Call to prayer: Play "Send Me an Angel," by Scorpions.

The first test of faith—*The Penitent Person Will Pass:* Play the *Last Crusade* clip of the first test of faith.

Ask the previously chosen teen to read Matt. 9:20–22 (humility before God).

After the reading, take time for quiet reflection.

Invite all to read the following prayer from their prayer sheet:

Teach me to walk humbly before you, Lord.
Let me never place myself before your will.
Give me the courage to admit my sins and failings,
and seek your precious gift of forgiveness.

The second test of faith—*Walking in the Footsteps of the Word:* Play the *Last Crusade* clip of the second test of faith.

Ask the previously chosen reader to read Matt. 4:18–20 ("'Come with me'").

After the reading, take time for quiet reflection.

Invite all to read the following prayer from their prayer sheet:

Teach me to walk in your footsteps, Lord,
even when it might not be the same path others choose.
When I stumble and fall, lead me to your word,
and guide my footsteps back toward you.

The third test of faith—*A Leap of Faith Will Prove Our Worth:* Play the *Last Crusade* clip of the third test of faith.

Ask the previously chosen teen to read Mark 6:7–12 ("'Don't take anything with you'").

After the reading, take time for quiet reflection.

Invite all to read the following prayer from their prayer sheet:

Lord, help me to see that even the impossible
is possible with you in my life.
Give me the gift of faith to rise above my doubts
and know you will carry me over the chasms in my life.

Closure: Pray together the Lord's Prayer.

12
Miscellaneous Prayer:
Prayers That Defy a Category

"Miscellaneous prayer" encompasses creative prayer suggestions that don't seem to fit into any of the other categories in this book.

Prayer Starters

1. As an alternative to attaching prayers to helium-filled balloons and letting them go, here is an idea that is both environmentally sound and uplifting: write original prayers on kites and send them skyward during a March prayer service.

2. Arrange for the teens to set up a dial-a-prayer service using a parish phone line. The service could run during the evening, when an answering machine usually takes calls. The teens could change the prayer message or words of inspiration for each day or week.

3. If your group is into rap, use it as a form of prayer for an entire prayer service. Rap the songs, readings, petitions, shared prayer—everything.

4. Have a "pasta and prayer" night: Everyone brings a single serving of a pasta dish along with a prayer to exchange with another person. It

can be challenging to find prayers suggested by the different types of pasta.

5. As an adaptation of the "add-on stories" game, start a prayer and pass it around the prayer circle verbally from one person to another, with each person adding to the prayer before passing it along to the next person.

6. Use the cooking, dyeing, and hiding of Easter eggs as part of a prayer service on the Trinity. An egg is a perfect symbol for the Trinity: the yolk, the white, and the shell are each different, but only together do they make up an egg.

7. Use prayer clues for a scavenger hunt around the parish complex and grounds.

8. Teach the teens how to make fortune cookies, and place a scriptural passage or a short prayer inside each one. Give the cookies out during a prayer service on "placing your fortune with Jesus Christ."

9. While on a long road trip with your group, challenge the teens to collect bumper sticker phrases and link them together to create a prayer solely out of those phrases. A variation on this is to use slogans from roadside billboards.

10. Exchange names at the beginning of December for "secret Santas" within your group. Instead of secretly leaving small gifts throughout the month, the Santas should leave scriptural passages, prayers, holy cards, and other religious items. Do not reveal the Santas' secret identities until after Christmas.

11. Carve pumpkins and place lighted candles inside of them for display during a prayer service on letting the light of Christ shine through each one of us.

12. Challenge the teens, in small groups, to create "prayer-mercials" (catchphrases) from the ads or jingles for common products. For example, Cheer Free detergent could become "Sin Free." Ask each group to share its prayer-mercials with the rest of the groups.

13. Why not lip-sync the words to a favorite church song?

14. Pretend that your group is visited by a being from another planet. How can you explain some of the things your group does when it prays? Ask a visitor to role-play the alien and trigger an interesting debate on "why we pray the way we pray."

Some Favorite Miscellaneous Prayers

Many of my favorite prayer experiences have already been relayed in the preceding pages of this book, but I have a few more that I would like to share with you:

Doodle Prayer

Hang large sheets of poster paper around your meeting space. Invite the group to draw doodles on them. Challenge the teens to find the prayers in the doodles. Some examples of doodles with their corresponding prayers follow:

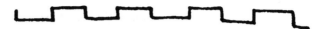

Dear God, help me to get through the ups and downs in my life.

Dear God, I feel like I am going around in circles. Please help me to straighten out.

Dear God, the things I have done make me feel like a giant knot inside. Please forgive me.

(Adapted from Betsy Caprio, *Experiments in Prayer,* pp. 88–89)

Marble Prayer

Hand out a marble to each person. Ask everyone to take their marble and hold it tightly in one hand. Tell them that the marble represents the unique individual that we hold inside ourselves. Sometimes we carefully protect and conceal our true self so no one else can see it, just as we hold the marble tightly in our fist.

Next, ask the teens to open their fist and let their marble sit in the palm of their hand. Explain that if they are not careful, the marble will roll out of their hand and drop to the floor. Reflect that just as with our hand, we take a risk when we open ourselves to others. We do not know if others will laugh at or dismiss or accept our true self. Yet we can never grow as a person unless we are able to share our true self.

Pray the following prayer:

Let us pray that God will give us the strength to open our heart and mind to God and one another. Let us share our true self with one another. We ask this through Christ, our Lord. Amen.

Yarn Web Prayer

Purchase or prepare a ball of multicolored yarn for this prayer.

Begin the prayer by holding on to the open end of the string of the ball of yarn and passing the ball to the person next to you. Ask that each person share a prayer and then pass the ball of yarn to another person anywhere in the circle, and make sure that everyone holds on to their place on the string of yarn as they pass the ball along.

Explain that the yarn's many colors symbolize that though we are very different from one another, we are all one in Jesus Christ. We may each have different needs and concerns, but we must work together as a community to support and encourage each other.

(Adapted from Marilyn and Dennis Benson, *Hard Times Catalog for Youth Ministry*, p. 212)

"Waters of Peace" Prayer

This prayer works best in prayer services or retreats in which the young people are from several different parishes.

Prepare for the prayer by asking a representative from each parish to bring a small bottle of holy water from their parish.

While everyone sings the song "Peace Is Flowing Like a River," invite the parish representatives to come forward and combine their water in a bowl as a sign that we are all one in the Lord through baptism.

Conduct a renewal of the baptismal promises using the water from the bowl to sprinkle on the teens or for them to dip their hands into. They can also bless themselves with the water as they leave, as a sign of their baptismal commitment.

"People Are Like Bread" Prayer

Write prayers of petition and attach them to different kinds of bread to symbolize the people for whom prayers will be offered. For example, shortbread could symbolize young people, while saltines could represent elderly people. Quick bread could be a symbol for all those who are in a hurry in our world, and nutbread for all those the world has called crazy for their ideas that go against the system.

The bread and petitions can be the centerpiece of a prayer service on being bread for the world, or they can be the petitions during an agape prayer service.

Popcorn Prayer

Use a popcorn popper with a clear cover on it. Have some popcorn kernels in it, ready to be popped.

Give each person a kernel of popcorn to feel and look at close up. Then call for everyone to add their kernel to those already in the popper.

Pop the popcorn while all watch. Reflect with the group on the transforming power of God—how God helps us break through the hardness of our outer shell to reveal the goodness and beauty inside.

(Adapted from Barbara L. Black and John M. Paulett, *Pentecost, Peanuts, Popcorn, and Prayer*, pp. 79–80)

Modern Parable Prayers

Think of commercials that use slogans or rhymes to sell products, and make the slogans or rhymes into a prayer parable. For example, a parable might be "The Kingdom of God Is Like a Bottle of Coke."

You could build a prayer service around the different slogans Coca-Cola has had for its product over the years and how those slogans describe the Kingdom of God: "It's the real thing." "Coke adds life." "Things go better with Coke." "Have a Coke and a smile." "Coke is it!" The Kingdom of God is real. It adds a lot to life here on earth and in the hereafter. Everything goes better when we are building the Kingdom. The Kingdom in action makes us smile. And it is the only way to go!

(The example is based on Daryl Olszewski, *Balloons! Candy! Toys! And Other Parables for Storytellers,* pp. 41–42.)

"One Body, Many Parts" Prayer

This activity is a way to pray a scriptural passage using drama.

Ask several of the people in your group to act out 1 Cor. 12:12–27 (one body with many parts). Assign each actor to be one of the parts of the body. One person can be the ears, another the feet, and so on. The body parts are to enter the stage area one at a time, acting out their role for the audience, then taking their place in the center as part of the body. This continues until all the parts are joined together to form one body.

If performing this for a large crowd, you may want to use props to make the body parts more visible to those sitting in the last row. For example, the "feet" could each hold a giant foot or have one attached to themselves.

(Based on Floyd Shaffer and Penne Sewall, *Clown Ministry,* pp. 65–68)

"Bubbles and Creation" Prayer

This activity is a way to pray about the wonders of God's creation.

For quiet time, give each teen a bottle of bubbles and encourage everyone to try different ways of blowing bubbles. Challenge them to discover what the bubbles can tell us about God's creation. Some examples follow:
• God's creation is fragile and must be handled with care.
• If we look close enough, we can see ourselves.
• We too are part of creation.

Allow time for the teens to share their discoveries with the entire group after the quiet time is over.

(Adapted from Joani Schultz, *Youth Ministry Cargo,* pp. 113–114)

Sponge Meditation

This activity can be used as a reflection exercise during a prayer service.

Prepare beforehand by cutting two sponges into several small pieces and finding a large drinking glass.

To begin the activity, ask the group to think of all the things that keep them busy and take up a lot of their time. Place one piece of sponge into the glass for each thing the group names, until the entire glass is full and there is no room for more sponges. Then pour water into the glass to illustrate how God is still able to find a place in our busy lives and is part of everything we do.

"Building the Kingdom" Prayer

Draw a large heart on a piece of pasteboard and place it on the floor in the center of the prayer space. Give each teen a Lego block.

Ask the teens to think of one way they can build the Kingdom of God and to make up a prayer that expresses it—for example, "Lord, help me to be more generous with my time."

Ask the teens to offer their prayer as they place their block around the pasteboard heart, building a visual Kingdom of God from their offerings of love and service.

Books with Prayer Ideas

Black, Barbara L., and John M. Paulett. *Pentecost, Peanuts, Popcorn, and Prayer.* New York: William H. Sadlier, 1982.

Caprio, Betsy. *Experiments in Prayer.* Notre Dame, IN: Ave Maria Press, 1973.

Cavanaugh, Brian. *The Sower's Seeds: One Hundred Inspiring Stories for Preaching, Teaching, and Public Speaking.* Mahwah, NJ: Paulist Press, 1990.

Fahy, Mary. *The Tree That Survived the Winter.* Mahwah, NJ: Paulist Press, 1989.

Fulghum, Robert. *All I Really Need to Know I Learned in Kindergarten.* New York: Villard Books, 1988.

———. *It Was on Fire When I Lay Down on It.* New York: Ballantine Books, 1991.

Girzone, Joseph F. *Joshua.* New York: Macmillan Publishing Company, 1987.

———. *Joshua and the Children.* New York: Macmillan Publishing Company, 1989.

Koch, Carl, ed. *Dreams Alive: Prayers by Teenagers.* Winona, MN: Saint Mary's Press, 1991.

Link, Mark. *The Psalms for Today: Praying an Old Book in a New Way.* Valencia, CA: Tabor Publishing, 1989.

Link, Mark, comp. *You: Prayer for Beginners and Those Who Have Forgotten How.* Niles, IL: Argus Communications, 1976.

Loder, Ted. *Guerrillas of Grace: Prayers for the Battle.* San Diego: LuraMedia, 1984.

Paulus, Trina. *Hope for the Flowers.* New York: Paulist Press, 1972.

Reutemann, Charles. *Let's Pray! Fifty Services for Praying Communities.* Winona, MN: Saint Mary's Press, 1975.

———. *Let's Pray/2.* Winona, MN: Saint Mary's Press, 1982.

Roche, Luane. *The Proud Tree.* Liguori, MO: Liguori Publications, 1981.

Acknowledgments (*continued*)

Unless otherwise noted, the scriptural quotations in this book are from the Good News Bible: The Bible in Today's English Version (New York: American Bible Society, 1979). New Testament copyright © 1976 by the American Bible Society. Used by permission.

Scriptural quotations designated as NRSV are from the New Revised Standard Version of the Bible, copyright © 1989 by the Division of Christian Education of the National Council of the Churches of Christ in the United States of America, and are used by permission. All rights reserved.

The poem excerpt on page 7 is from "God . . . Are You There?" in *Guerrillas of Grace: Prayers for the Battle,* by Ted Loder, copyright © 1984 by LuraMedia, Inc., San Diego, California. Used by permission.

Prayer starter 11 on page 14 comes from a banner designed by the Saint Thomas More youth group, Allentown, Pennsylvania, for the 1988 Youth Day, Diocese of Allentown.

Song reflections found in chapter 2, and the "Creed for Life," on page 35, were published previously in "Find Faith in Music" and "Learning to Be Pro-Life," respectively, by Maryann Hakowski, in the *A.D. Times,* the newspaper for the Diocese of Allentown.

The prayer by Sheri Harrison, on page 39, is taken from *Dreams Alive: Prayers by Teenagers,* ed. Carl Koch, FSC (Winona, MN: Saint Mary's Press, 1991). Copyright © 1991 by Saint Mary's Press. All rights reserved.

Prayer starter 11 on page 49 is adapted from Rally for Mary, Diocese of Allentown, 1986.

Prayer starter 1 on page 54 comes from a Lenten project by the youth group of Saint Mary's Parish in Kutztown, Pennsylvania.

Teens from the Catholic Youth Council of Pennsylvania assisted in developing the prayer service "Discovering Christ in Each Other," on pages 56–58.

The prayer service "What Do You Need for the Journey?" on pages 68–70, is loosely adapted from a prayer service celebrated at the annual youth ministers' retreat, Archdiocese of Baltimore, 1991.

The story "The Starfish," on page 74, is titled "Make a Difference, #2" in *The Sower's Seeds: One Hundred Inspiring Stories for Preaching, Teaching, and Public Speaking,* by Brian Cavanaugh, TOR (Mahwah, NJ: Paulist Press, 1990), page 26. Copyright © 1990 by Brian Cavanaugh, TOR. Used by permission of the publisher.

The story "Bundles of Worries, Bundles of Blessings," on pages 75–76, is excerpted from *A Piece of the Wind and Other Stories to Tell,* by Ruthilde Kronberg and Patricia C. McKissack. Copyright © 1990 by Ruthilde Kronberg and Patricia C. McKissack. Reprinted by arrangement with Harper San Francisco, a division of HarperCollins Publishers, Inc.

The story "Two Brothers," on page 76, is reprinted from *An Experience Named Spirit,* by John Shea, with permission from the Thomas More Press, Chicago, IL 60606.

The story "View from the Balcony," on pages 78–79, is an Associated Press news story from 16 March 1992. Used by permission.

Prayer starter 11 on page 88 is adapted from a prayer service at an October 1991 meeting of Region III of the National Federation for Catholic Youth Ministry.

The Doodle Prayer, on pages 88–89, is adapted from *Experiments in Prayer,* by Betsy Caprio (Notre Dame, IN: Ave Maria Press, 1973), pages 88–89. Copyright © by Betsy Caprio. Used by permission of the author.

The Marble Prayer, on page 89, is adapted from Sr. Andre Dembowski, Sunrise Retreat, Fatima Center, Scranton, Pennsylvania.

The Yarn Web Prayer, on page 89, is adapted from an activity developed by Monica Brown in *Hard Times Catalog for Youth Ministry,* page 212. Copyright © 1982 by Marilyn and Dennis Benson. Published by Group Books, Box 481, Loveland, CO 80539. Used by permission of the authors.

The "People Are Like Bread" Prayer, on page 90, is adapted from a prayer service held at a gathering of Pennsylvania retreat directors in 1988.

The Popcorn Prayer, on page 90, is an adaptation from *Pentecost, Peanuts, Popcorn, and Prayer,* by Barbara L. Black and John M. Paulett (Villa Maria, PA: The Center for Learning). Copyright © 1988 by the Center for Learning, Villa Maria, Pennsylvania. Used by permission.

The example for Modern Parable Prayers, on page 91, is adapted from "The Kingdom of God Is Like a Bottle of Coke" in *Balloons! Candy! Toys! And Other Parables for Storytellers,* by Daryl Olszewski (San Jose, CA: Resource Publications, 1986), pages 41–42. Copyright © 1986 by Resource Publications, Inc., 160 East Virginia Street, Number 290, San Jose, CA 95112. Used by permission.

The "One Body, Many Parts" Prayer, on page 91, is adapted by permission from *Clown Ministry,* copyright © 1984 by Floyd Shaffer and Penne Sewall. Published by Group Books, Box 481, Loveland, CO 80539.

The "Bubbles and Creation" Prayer, on page 91, is adapted by permission from *Youth Ministry Cargo,* copyright © 1986 by Joani Schultz and dozens of contributors. Published by Group Books, Box 481, Loveland, CO 80539.

The "Building the Kingdom" Prayer, on page 92, is from a closing prayer service, the Leadership Training Program, Department of Youth Ministry, Diocese of Allentown. Sr. Barbara Lester assisted with the planning.

Other Books by Maryann Hakowski

Resources for Youth Retreats

Resources for Youth Retreats is a two-volume series that contains multiple resources for conducting one-day, overnight, or weekend retreats for high school young people. Each volume contains selections for preparing retreats, retreat evaluation guides, meal menus, ideas for recruiting and training retreat teams, retreat-talk outlines and scripts, easily reproducible handouts for various exercises, plus many original retreat activities, easily accessed by way of a categorized index. For the inexperienced retreat director, the retreat activities, retreat outlines and scripts, and exercise handouts are combined into completely scheduled and detailed retreats—five retreats in each volume.

Vine & Branches 1   Vine & Branches 2

The five retreat themes in this volume are spirituality, confirmation, relationships, parables, and prayer.

The five retreat themes in this volume are Advent, social justice, nature, sacraments, and the person of Jesus.

Order from your local religious bookstore or from

Saint Mary's Press
702 TERRACE HEIGHTS
WINONA MN 55987-1320
USA